AJ Rockschool Academy Step-by-Step Guitar for Beginners Book 1

By
Alistair Jobson

Copyright © 2023 Alistair Jobson

All rights reserved.

 Visit the Website
www.ajrockschoolacademy.com

 Email:
www.info@ajrockschoolacademy.com

 View the YouTube Channel
AJROCKSCHOOLACADEMY

 Follow on Instagram
AJROCKSCHOOLACADEMY

 Follow on TikTok
AJROCKSCHOOLACADEMY

 Like on Facebook
AJROCKSCHOOLACADEMY

COPYRIGHT CONDITIONS

No part of this publication may be reproduced, distributed, or transmitted in any form or by any means, including photocopying, recording, or other electronic or mechanical methods, without the prior written permission of the publisher.

Image Credits: Images used in this book are sourced from Freepik.com by the following artists:@freepik, @brgfx, @macrovector, @upklyak, @rawpixel.com, @catalyststuff, @pikisuperstar, @macrovector_official, @pch.vector, @studio4rt, @alicia_mb @dgim-studio

ACKNOWLEDGMENTS

I want to thank my wife for her incredible help and support in writing this book.
I am also grateful to everyone else who cheered me on throughout this journey, and also
all the fantastic students I've taught over the past 26 years.
Thank you all so much! Alistair

List of Contents

Introduction	Page VI		
About Practice	Page VI		
Parts of the Guitar	Page 1	Super Spies are	Page 12
Holding a Guitar	Page 2	Chasing Pies	
The Pick/Plectrum	Page 3	Hats	Page 13
Holding a Pick/Plectrum	Page 3		
Holding down a note	Page 4	We're all Cats with Hats.	Page 13
		Be a Bee	Page 14
Finding the Notes	Page 5	Bee Yourself	Page 14
The Musical Alphabet	Page 6	Can this B	Page 15
The Staff/Stave	Page 6	more Spooky	
Treble Clef	Page 6	Scary Noise	Page 15
Notes on the Stave	Page 7	Racing Car	Page 16
Musical Notes	Page 8	Minim/Half Note Rest	Page 16
		Nearly Silent Song	Page 16
The 1st Note	Page 9	Tune of the Moon	Page 16
Easy to Play G	Page 10		
The 2nd Note	Page 10	The Note "C"	Page 17
The Note "A"	Page 10	I can C you	Page 17
Find Mr A	Page 11	"C" is the Magic Letter	Page 17
Find Mr G	Page 11	I C the Sea	Page 18
Mr G meets Mr A	Page 12	Smelly Feet	Page 18

The Note "D"	Page 19	Climbing Mountains	Page 29
So this is D	Page 19	Best game Ever!	Page 29
Go Tell the Aunties	Page 19		
If You See a Crocodile	Page 20	D Chord	Page 30
Song of Joy	Page 20	The Power of 4 Chords	Page 31
Lightly Row	Page 20	Write Your Own	Page 32
		Songwriting Continued.	Page 33
CHORDS	Page 21		
Easy G	Page 21	Tablature	Page 35
Easy Em	Page 22	Jingle Bells	Page 36
Easy C	Page 23	Eeee!	Page 37
Mix them UP!	Page 24	Bingo was his name!	Page 37
Buying Biscuits	Page 24	Pirates	Page 38
Three four time	Page 25	The Crotchet Rest	Page 39
Waltzing In!	Page 25	The Race	Page 40
Dotted Minim	Page 25	There They Go!	Page 40
Ring for 3	Page 25	Semibreve	Page 41
Row your Boat	Page 26	Long Time	Page 41
Barcarolle	Page 26	Oh When the Saints	Page 42
Musical tie	Page 27		
Who Ties the Tie?	Page 27	Quiz Answers	Page 43
Flowers from the North	Page 28	Music Award	Page 46
Muckle Massive	Page 29		

Even professional musicians started out as beginners!

Introduction

Welcome to "AJ Rock School Academy's Step-by Step Guitar for Beginners Book 1" the first in a series of guitar books where you will become equipped with the skills and knowledge to play your acoustic guitar.

In this book, I'll take you through the basics of playing acoustic guitar, reading music, interpreting chord boxes, and understanding tablature. It's an adventure that will unveil the secrets of music, allowing you to play your favourite songs and even create your own unique compositions.

No more daunting and confusing instructions – my step-by-step approach will make learning the acoustic guitar a breeze, making sure you progress at your own pace and have fun along the way.

Get ready to immerse yourself in the beauty of acoustic guitar, as we unlock the mysteries of music.

So, grab your acoustic guitar, tune those strings, and let's embark on an unforgettable journey of rhythm, melody, and harmony!

Practice

Becoming a great footballer or artist takes more than just owning the right equipment; PRACTICE is the key. Similarly, being amazing at video games doesn't happen overnight; it's about persistence and not giving up after a single try.

Learning guitar follows the same path, demanding time, patience, and effort, but the rewards are truly amazing.

Set aside daily or regular time to play your guitar and review your music – this is the secret to not only becoming good but achieving greatness as a player. Rock stars may appear effortless on stage, but the audience doesn't see the hours of dedication behind their performance.

You can achieve greatness too; it simply takes practice!

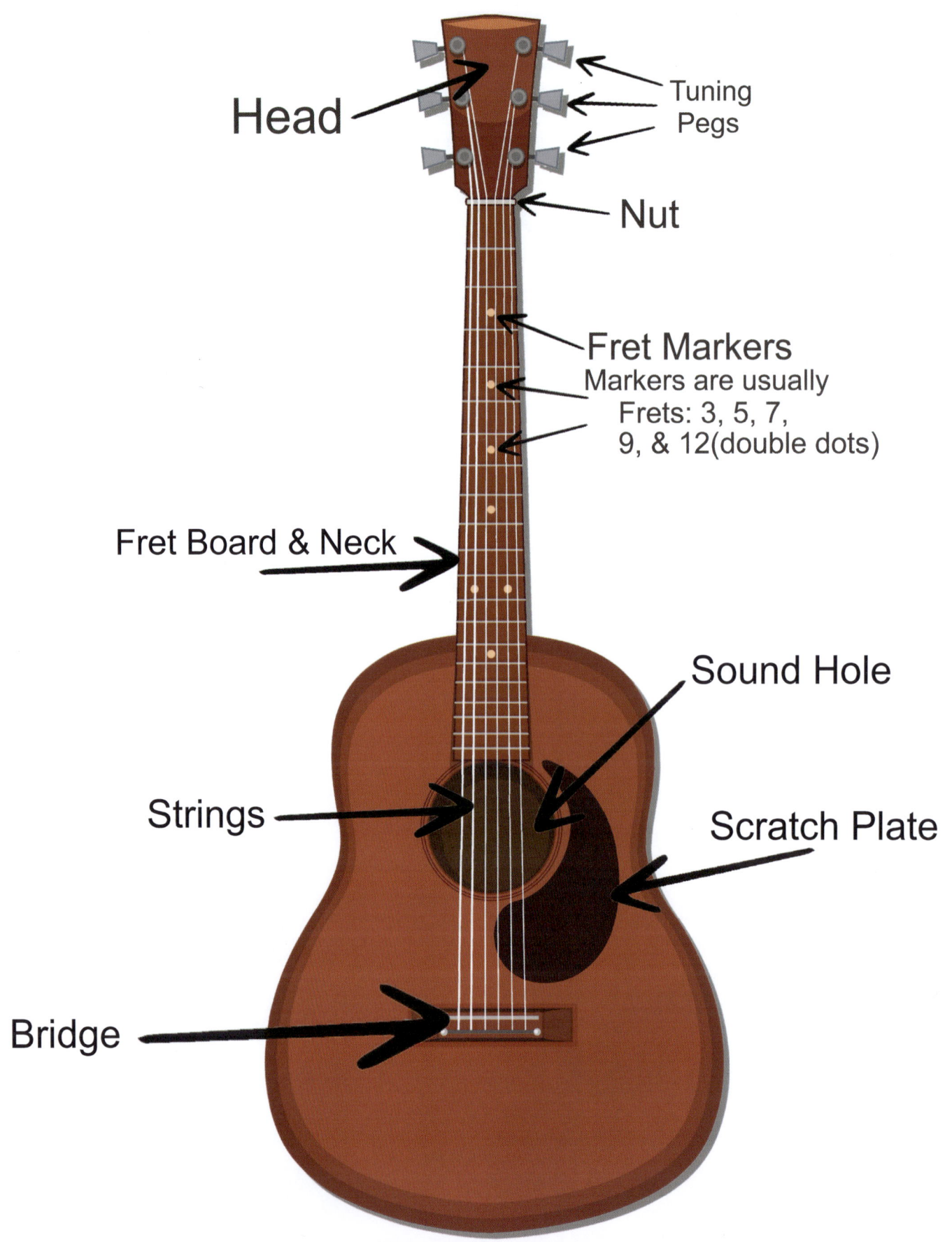

Holding a Guitar

The Pick/Plectrum

A plectrum, also known as a pick, is a small, triangular tool made of plastic, used to pluck or strum the strings of a guitar or other stringed instruments. It helps produce sound and control the tone and volume.

Holding a Pick/Plectrum

Hold the guitar pick between your thumb and index finger, pointed end towards the strings. Maintain a firm but relaxed grip, with a small portion of the pick extending out from your fingers.

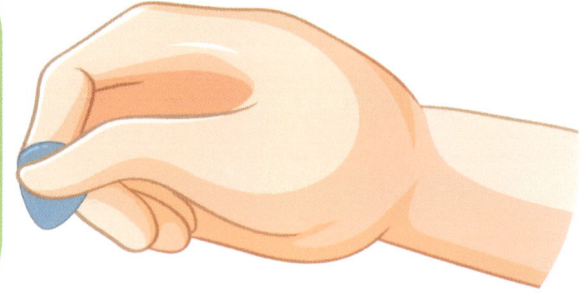

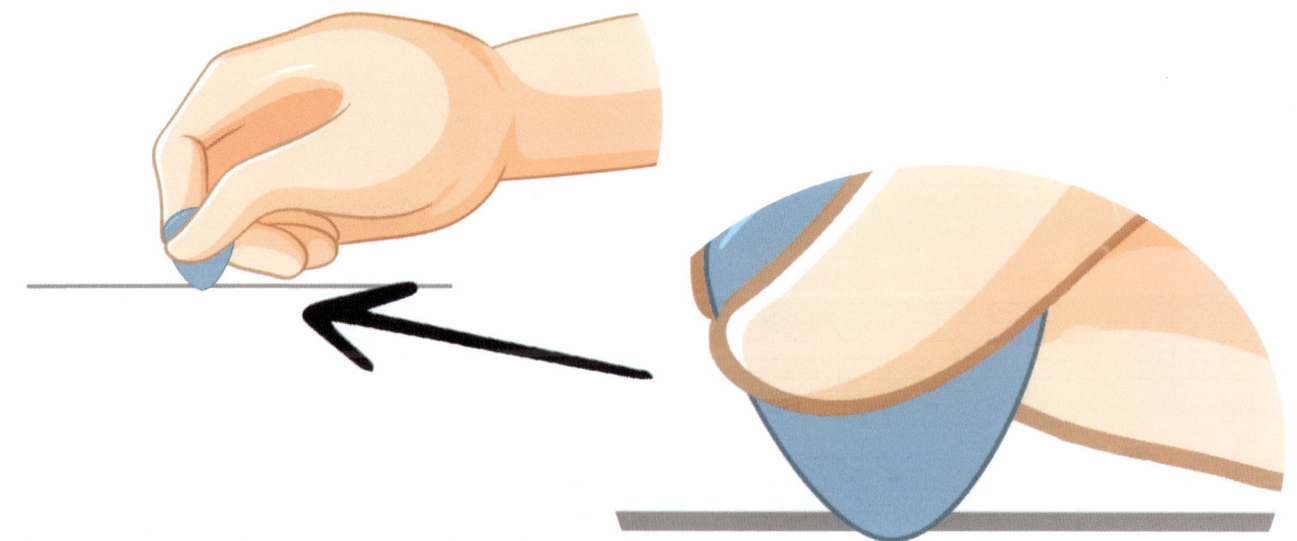

Use the very tip of the plectrum to play the string.

Holding down a note

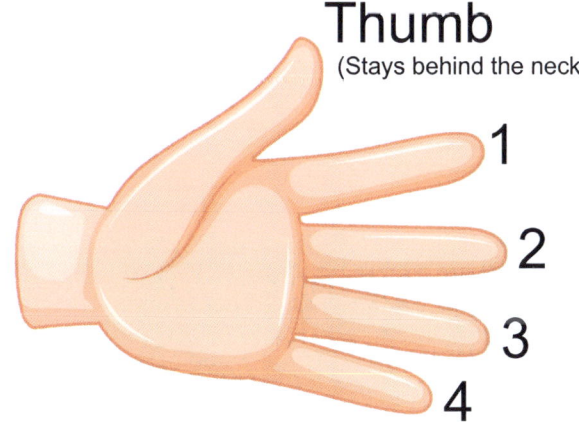

In guitar playing, the thumb is not counted as a finger for the fretting hand. It stays behind the neck while the fingers are numbered 1 to 4, starting from the index finger to the pinky finger.

To play a single note on the guitar, curve your hand around the neck and press your fingers at the edge of the desired fret, using the tips of your fingers. Avoid pressing directly on the metal fret wire.

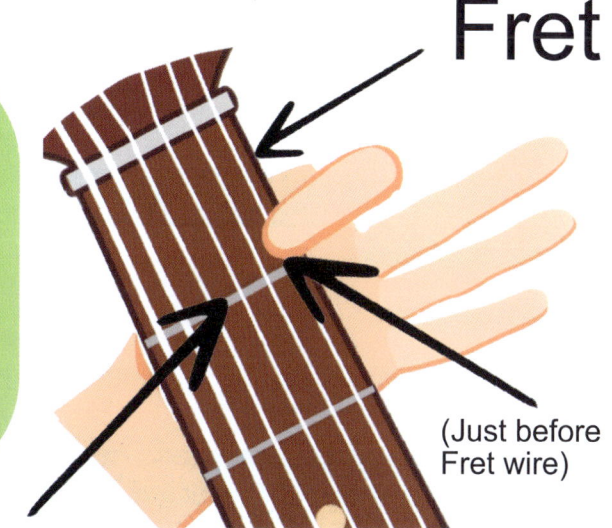

Finding the Notes

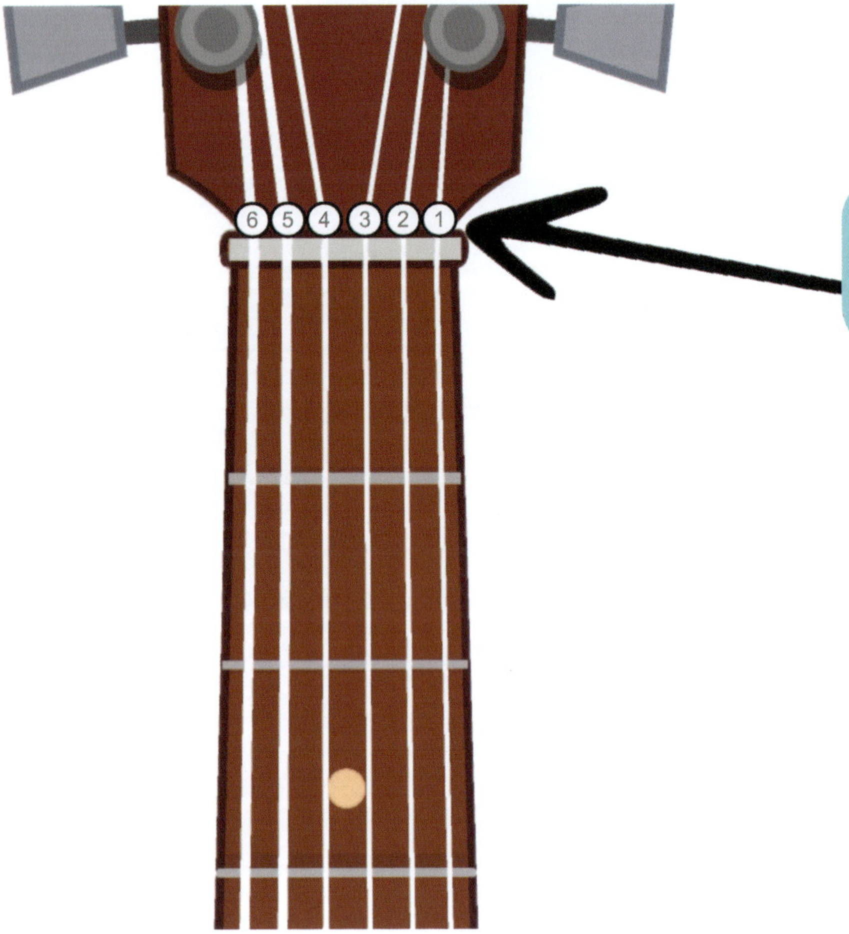

Strings are numbered 1 to 6. 6 is the thickest string & 1 the thinnest!

Each of these strings is tuned to a certain note (musical letter)! When a string is played on its own it is called an "Open String".

So here we have 6 Open Strings, playing the notes E A D G B E

The Musical Alphabet

Just as the regular alphabet has letters from A to Z, the musical alphabet has letters too, but instead of A to Z, it goes from A to G. These letters represent different musical notes.

The musical stave, or staff, is a set of lines and spaces that musicians use to write down and read music. It's like a musical playground where the notes have their special spots to rest and play.

The stave is made up of five lines and four spaces. It looks a bit like a ladder lying flat. The lines and spaces have different names and represent different musical notes.

The Stave/Staff

5 Lines

4 Spaces

Treble Clef

The treble clef is a musical symbol that helps us read and understand music. It looks like a fancy curly line. It's also sometimes called the "G clef" because it curls around the line that represents the note G.

When you see a treble clef at the beginning of a stave, it tells you the stave is meant for higher-pitched notes. It acts like a musical map, guiding you through the melody.

Notes on the Stave

On the previous page I mentioned the five lines and four spaces. Each one of these lines and spaces is a different note (musical letter). Here is what they are, and also a method to help you remember each line and space is for a different note.

Lines: **E**very **G**reen **B**us **D**rives **F**ast

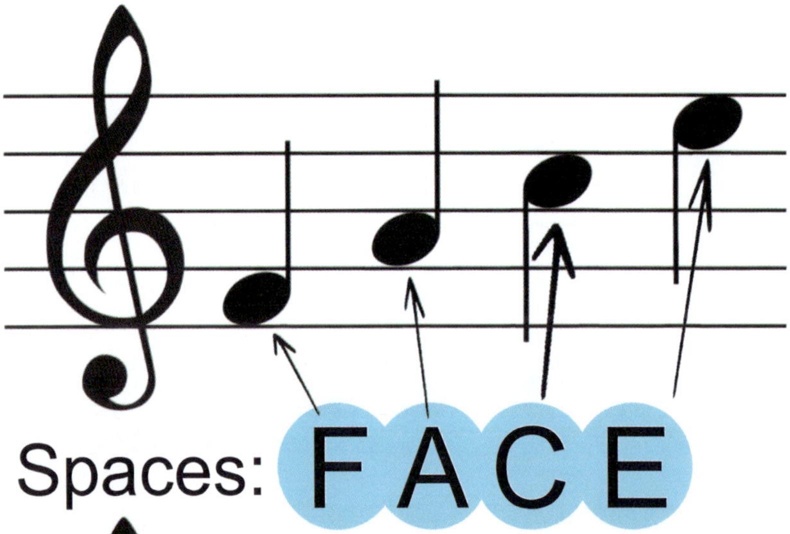

Spaces: FACE

Quiz Question 1
Can you name these notes?

Quiz answers at the back of the book

Musical Notes

Here are 4 different types of notes. They each have 2 names. Their traditional name and their modern name.

Note	Traditional Name	Modern Name	Note Length
♪	Quaver	8th Note	½ Beat
♩	Crotchet	¼ Note	1 Beat
♩ (half)	Minim	½ Note	2 Beats
𝅝	Semibreve	Whole Note	4 Beats

When a note changes how it looks, it is telling us how long you must let the note make a sound for. Each one of these notes last for a different amount of time.

Time Signature

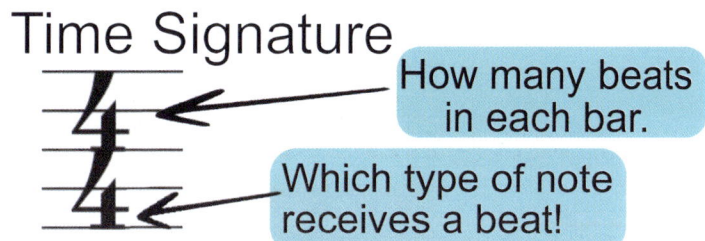

How many beats in each bar.

Which type of note receives a beat!

The 1st Note

On The Stave
"G" can be found on the 2nd line

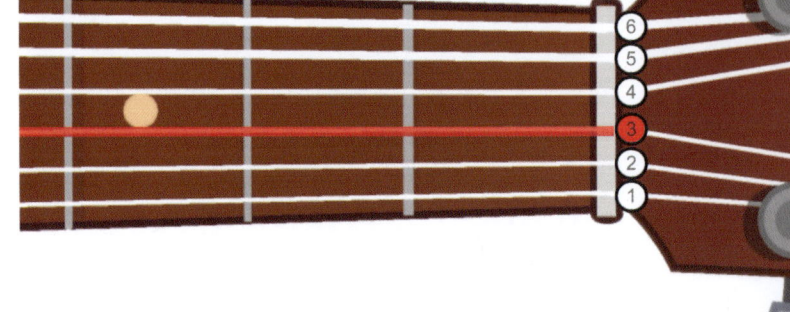

On The Guitar
The note "G" can be found by playing string 3 by itself. Use your thumb or a pick to play the notes below.

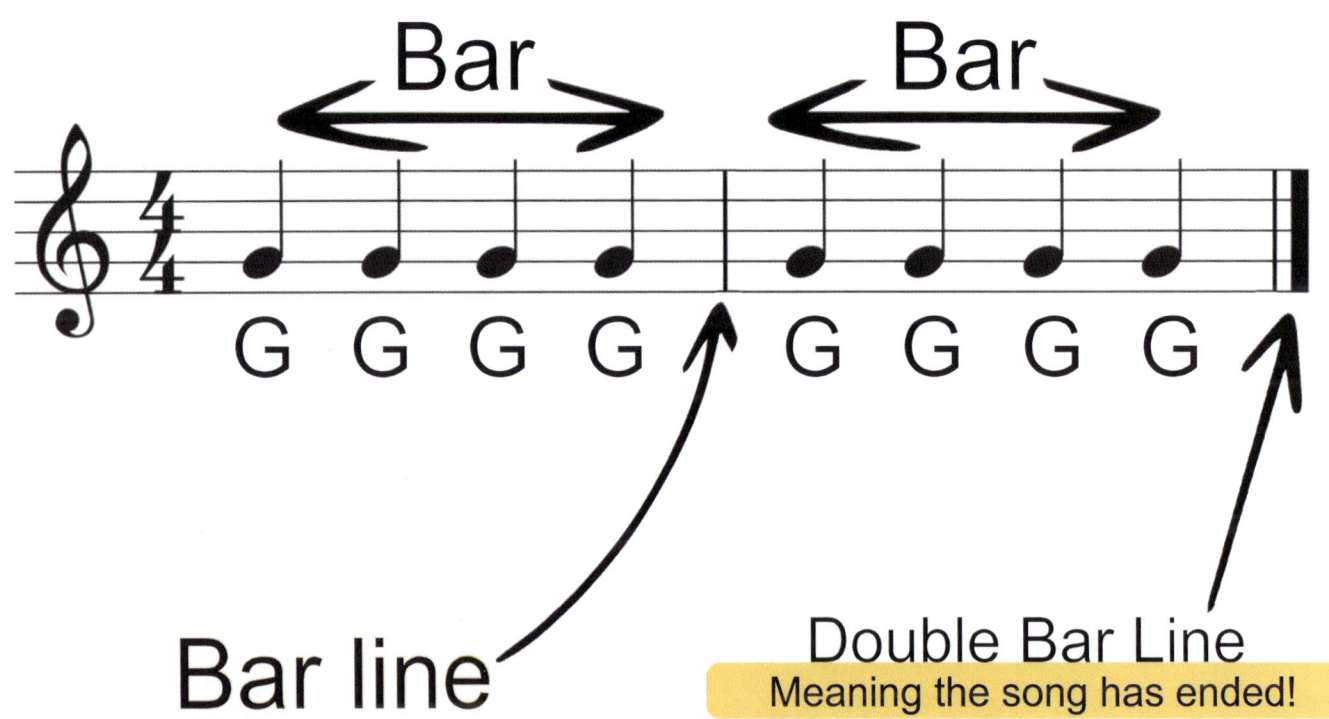

Bar line
Separates each bar, making music easier to read.

Double Bar Line
Meaning the song has ended!

Easy to Play G

4 beats in each bar, count along if you like.

The 2nd Note

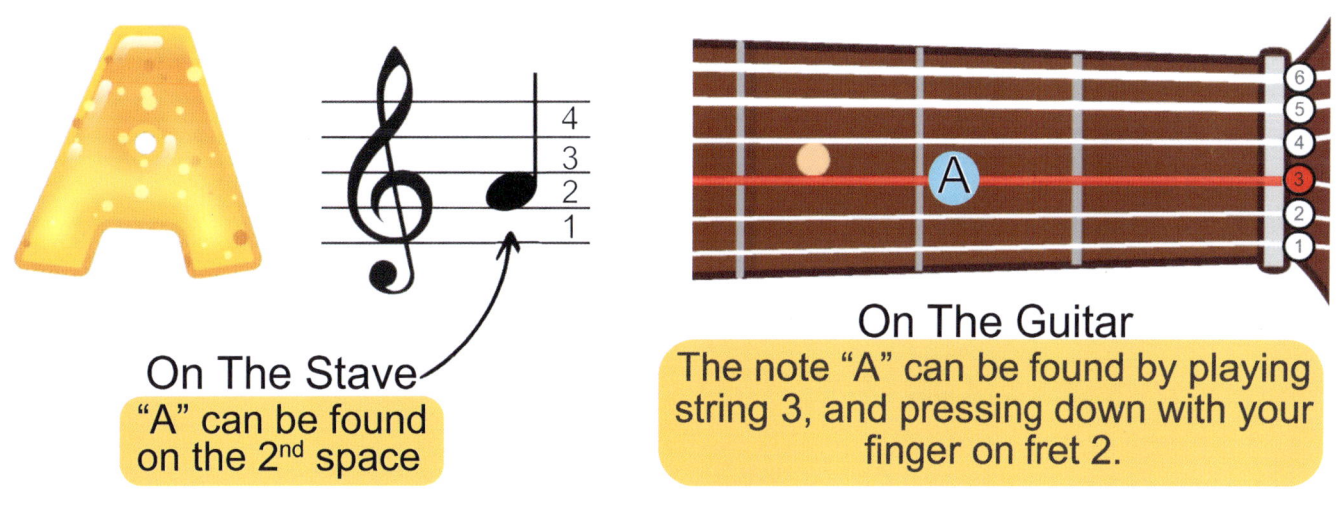

On The Stave
"A" can be found on the 2nd space

On The Guitar
The note "A" can be found by playing string 3, and pressing down with your finger on fret 2.

The Note A

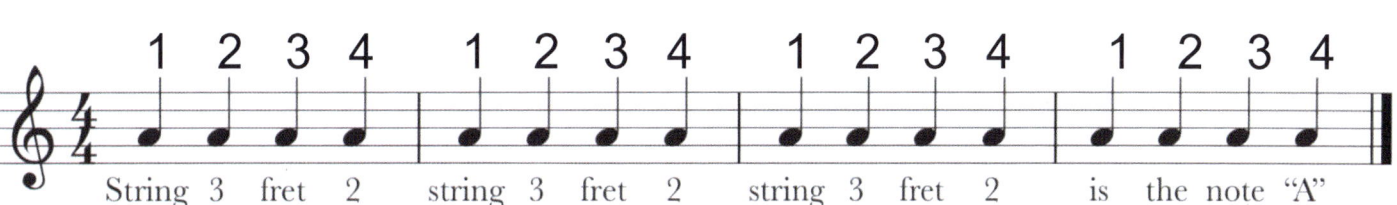

String 3 fret 2, string 3 fret 2, string 3 fret 2, is the note "A"

Well done! You can play 2 notes!

Quiz Question 2

Amongst lots of the same notes, can you find the A's and G's?

Find Mr A

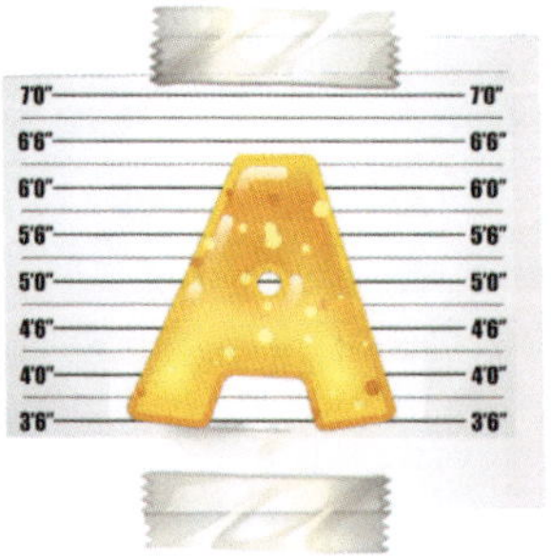

Find Mr G

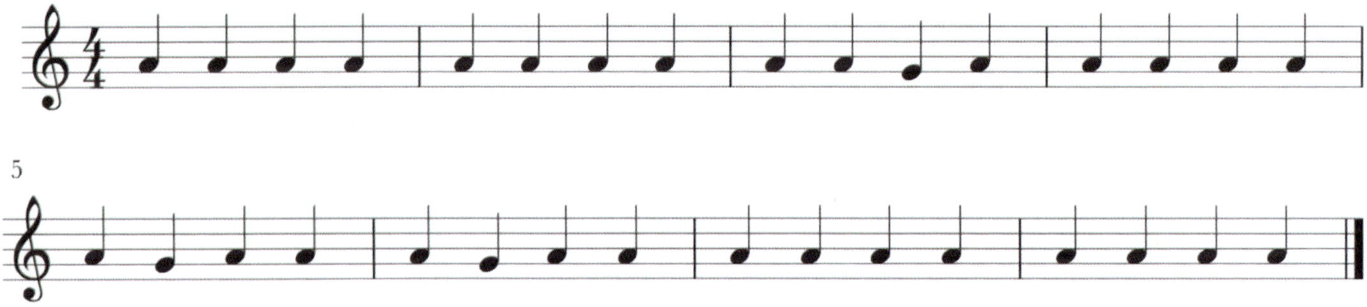

Quiz answers at the back of the book

Mr G meets Mr A

Now play G and A together

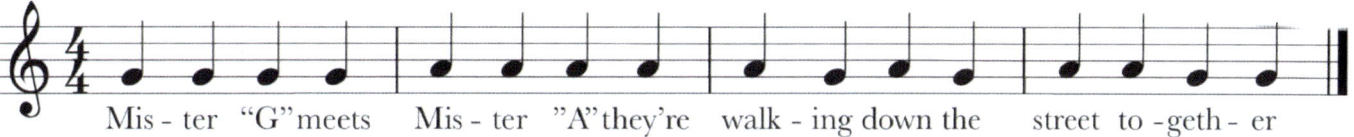
Mis - ter "G" meets Mis - ter "A" they're walk - ing down the street to - geth - er

Super Spies are Chasing Pies

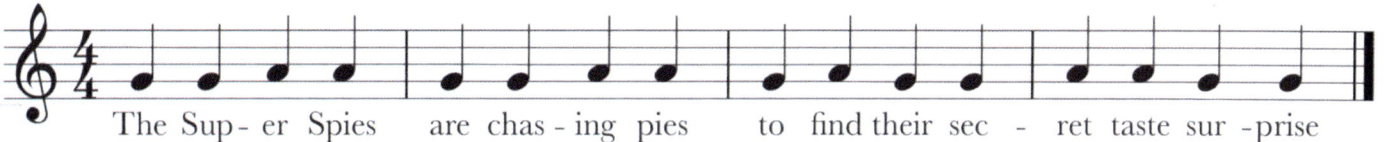
The Sup - er Spies are chas - ing pies to find their sec - ret taste sur - prise

Hats

Minim/Half Note
2 Beats

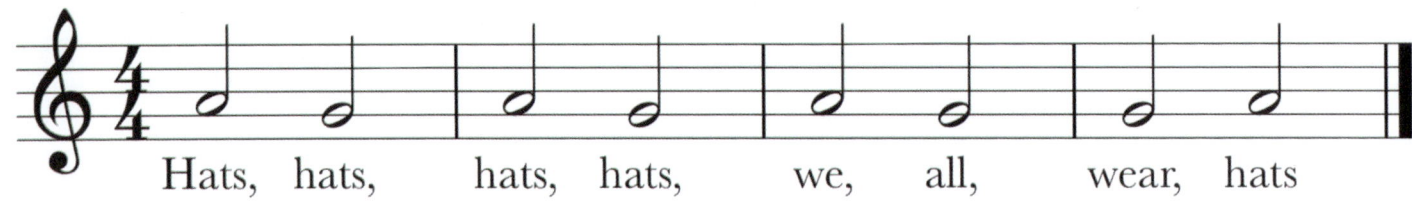

Hats, hats, hats, hats, we, all, wear, hats

> Just like changing a hat, if a note looks different, it just means it is played for a different amount of time. If it hasn't moved on the stave, it is still the same note.

We're all Cats with Hats

We're all cats with hats, when, we change how we look, it,

chang - es, how, long, we, will, sound, thank - you

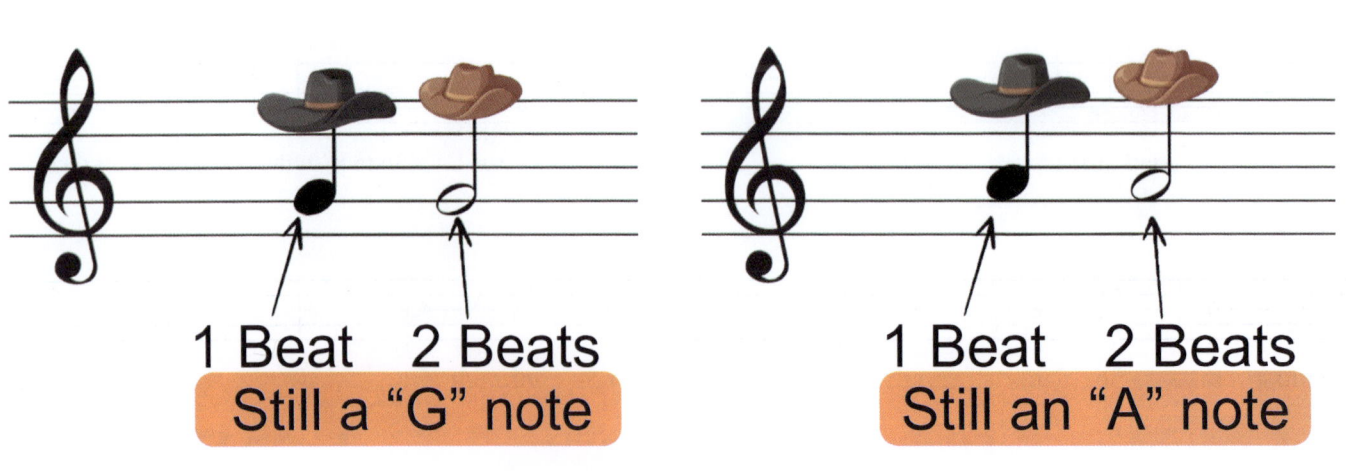

1 Beat   2 Beats   1 Beat   2 Beats
Still a "G" note   Still an "A" note

On The Stave
"B" can be found on the 3rd line of the stave.

On The Guitar
The note "B" can be found by playing string 2 by itself.

Be a Bee

Be, be, be a Bee be a be a bus-y Bee

Bee Yourself

Be your be your-self you should alw-ays be you

Quiz Question 3

Where can the note "B" be found on the guitar?

The Note "C"

On The Stave
"C" can be found on the 3rd space.

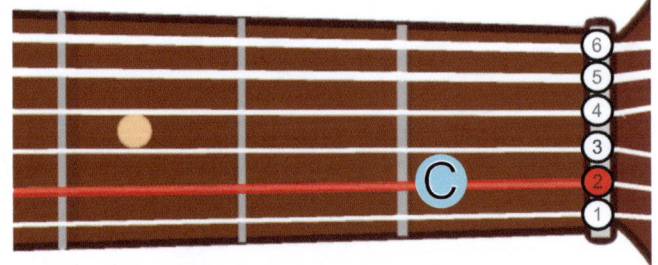

On The Guitar
The note "C" can be found by playing string 2, and pressing down with your finger on fret 1.

I can C you

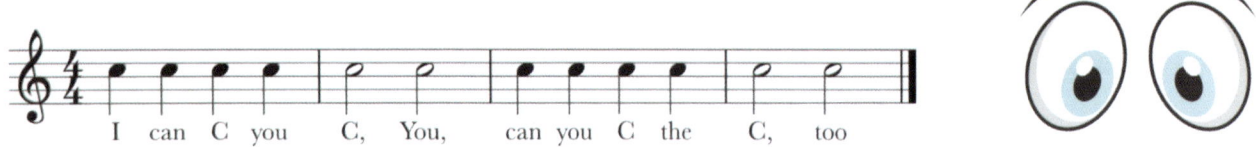

I can C you C, You, can you C the C, too

"C" is the Magic Letter

Why, do they say, that, C's the Ma-gic let-ter?

How, can it be a fact, when I've nev-er heard that?

I C the Sea

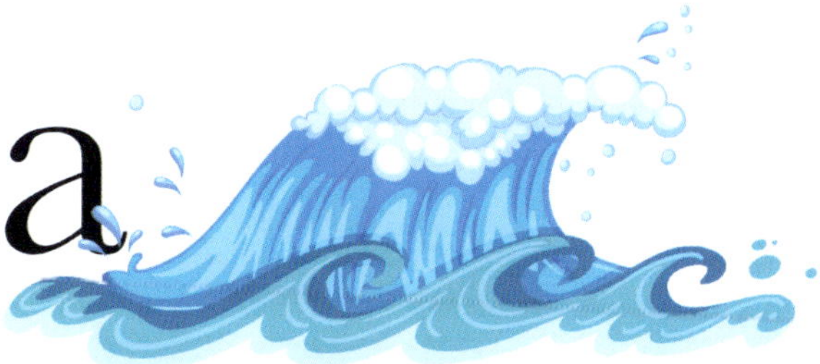

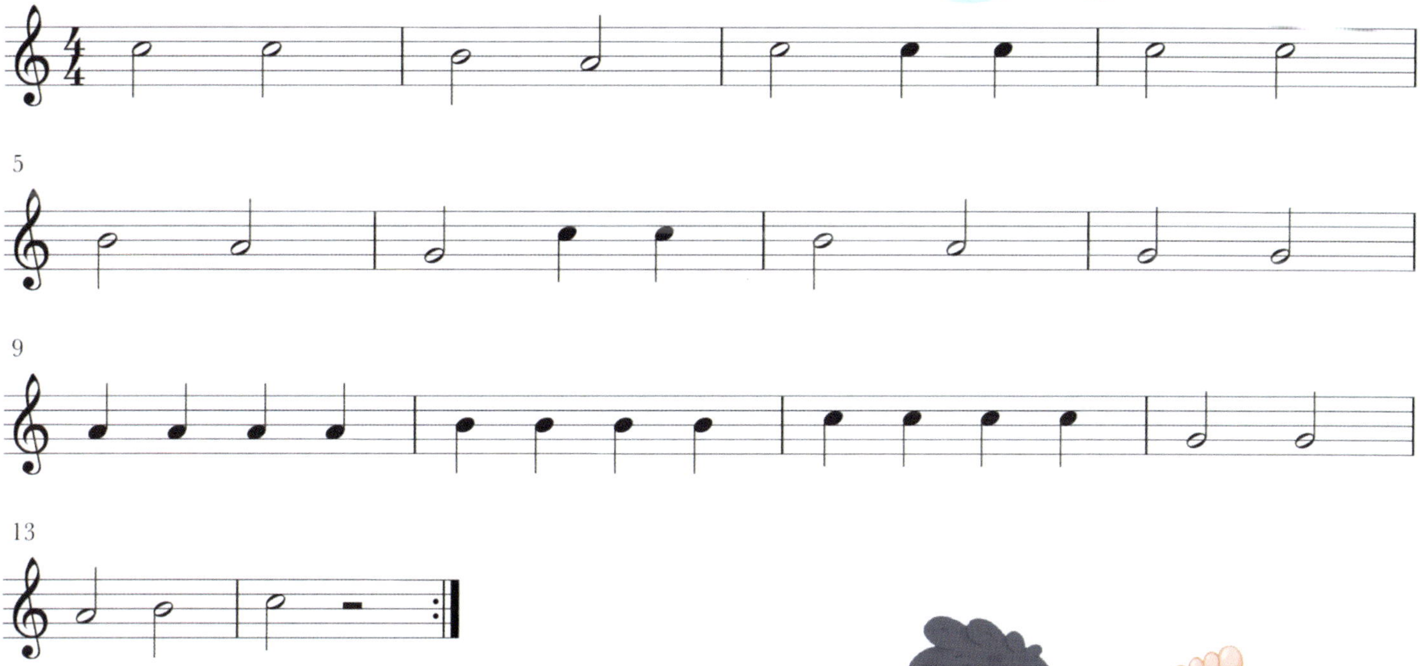

Smelly Feet

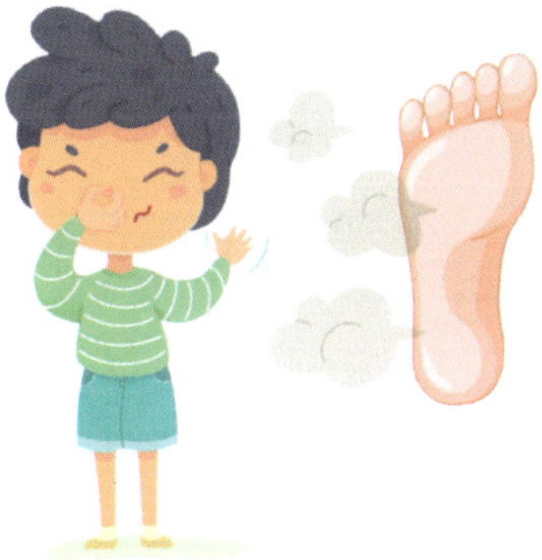

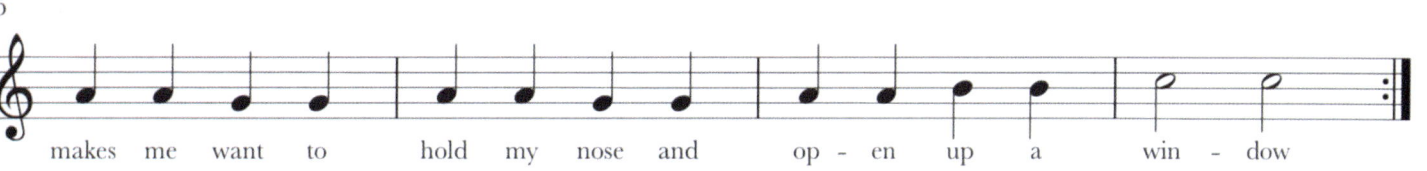

Can, you, smell, the, stink of smel - ly feet, yuck, makes me want to hold my nose and op - en up a win - dow

Quiz Question 4

What does the top number of the time signature mean?

The Note "D"

On The Stave
"D" can be found on the 4th line.

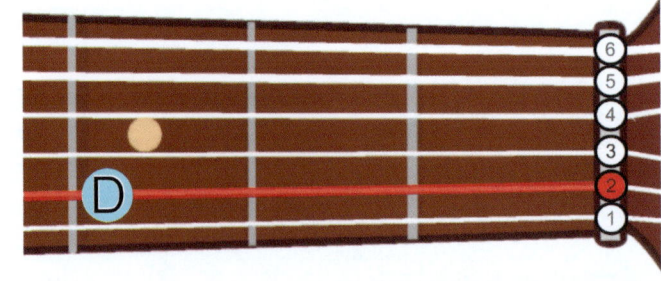

On The Guitar
The note "D" can be found by playing string 2, and pressing down with your finger on fret 3.

So this is D

D D this is D, D is String 2 and fret 3

Go Tell the Aunties

Go tell Aunt Nan - cy   go tell Aunt Hil - da
go tell Aunt Liz - zie, the grey goose has re - turned!

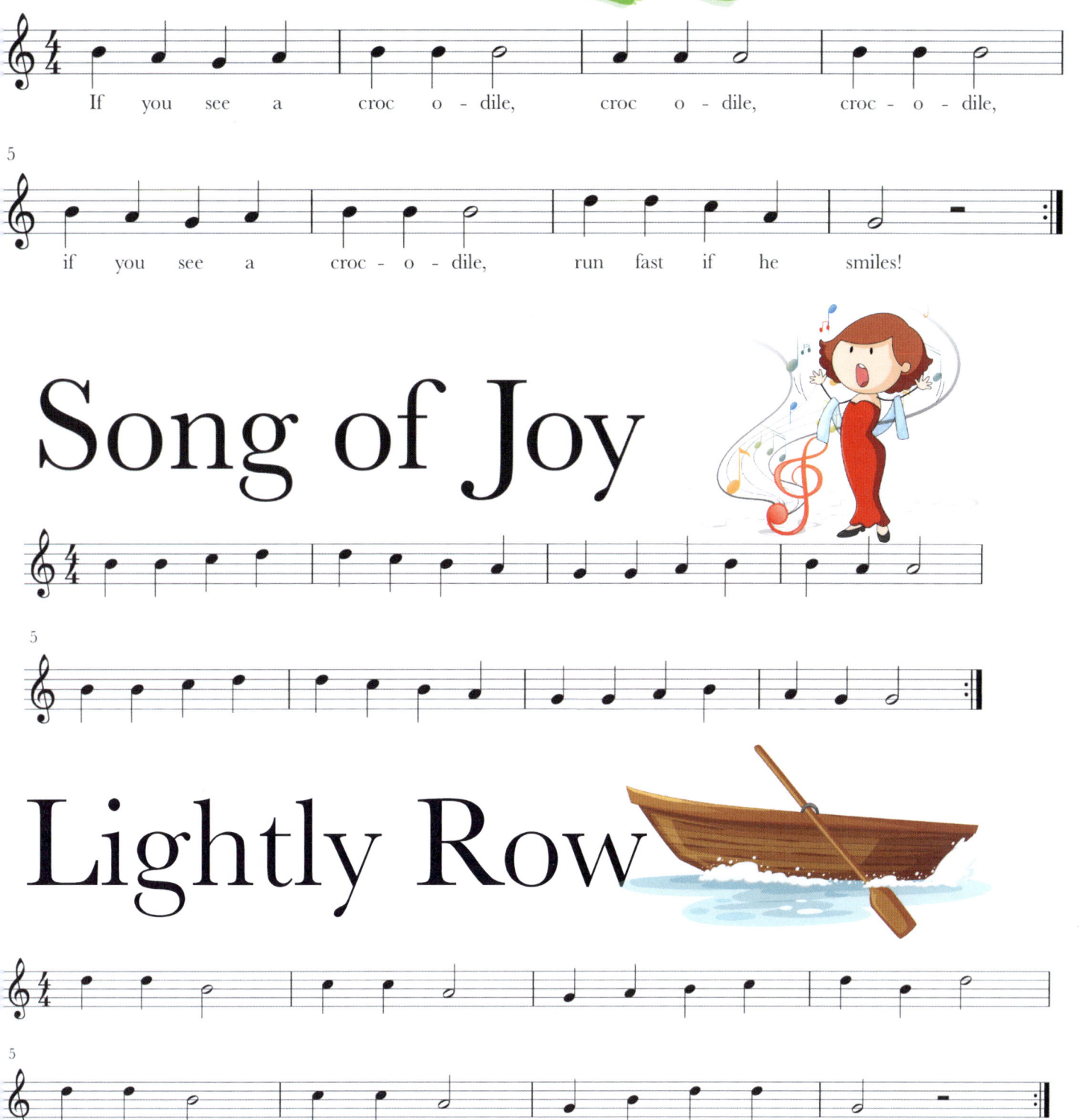

Chords

What is a Chord? — A chord is a collection of musical notes played together at the same time.

How do we play a chord on a guitar? — To play a chord on the guitar, you simply press your finger or fingers on certain strings (depending which chord you want to play) and **Strum** them (play those strings all at once).

How do I know which strings to press? — Chords are usually learnt using a chord box, which shows you where to press your fingers for each chord.

Easy G

First chord we will call Easy G! Press 3rd finger on string 1, fret 3.

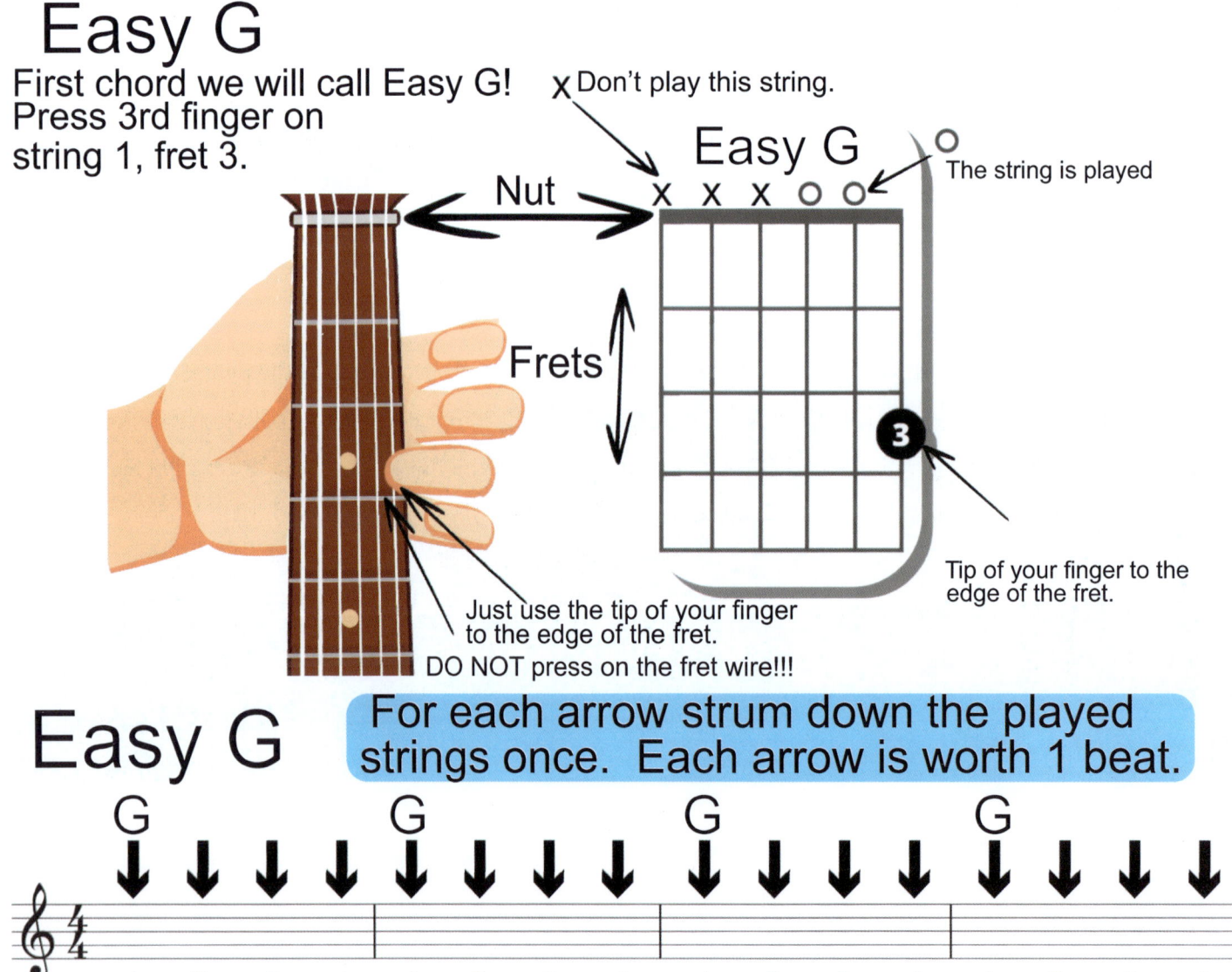

Easy Em

What is the m, in Em?

> The 'm' stands for minor. So this is an E minor chord. Chords without an 'm' written after e.g. 'E', or 'G' etc are major chords, written as just a letter on their own.

What is major, and what is minor?

> Put simply, major chords are happy sounding chords, while minor chords are sad sounding chords.

Great News!!!

Easy Em is 3 open strings, which means no fingers to press down. Just strum those 3 strings.

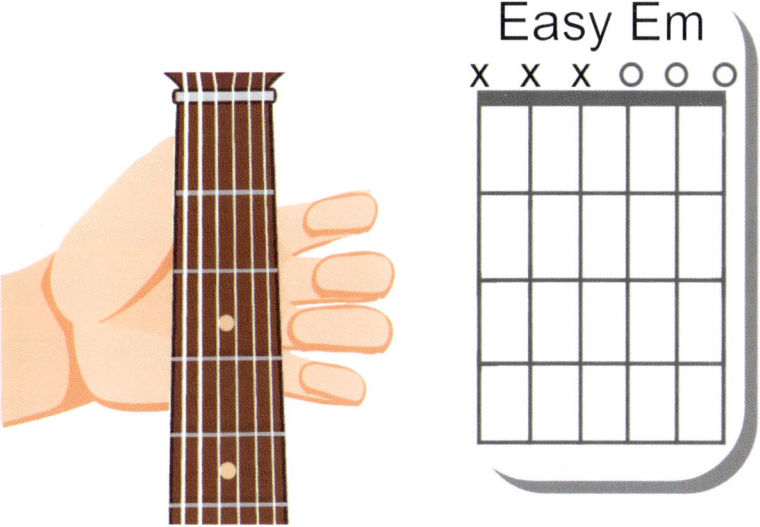

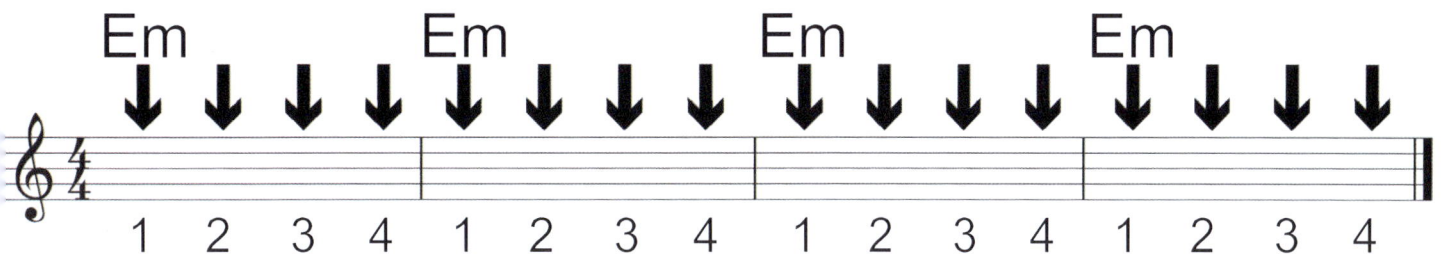

Easy C

Easy C
Press 1st finger on string 2, fret 1.

Note:
Arch your finger OVER string 1 to avoid muting string 1.

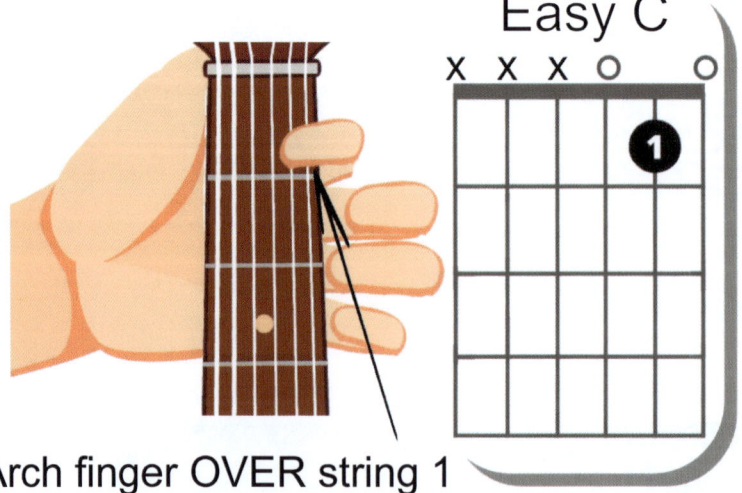

Arch finger OVER string 1

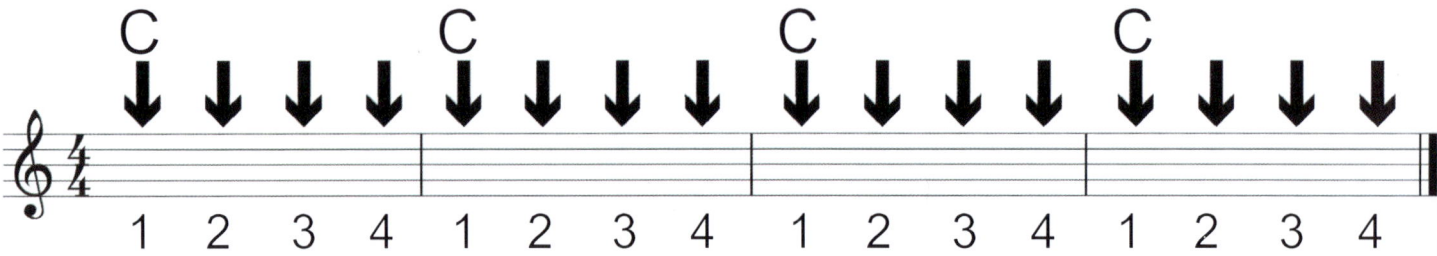

2 chord strum

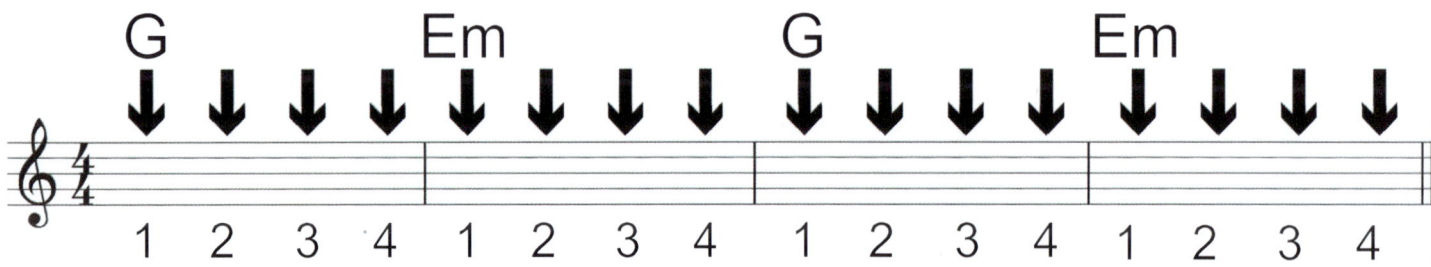

Now try them this way

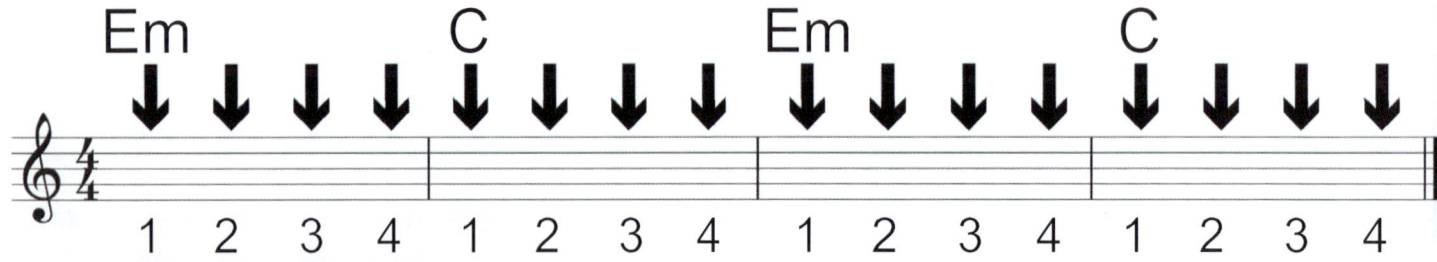

Quiz Question 5

Which string on the guitar is number 1?

Mix them UP!

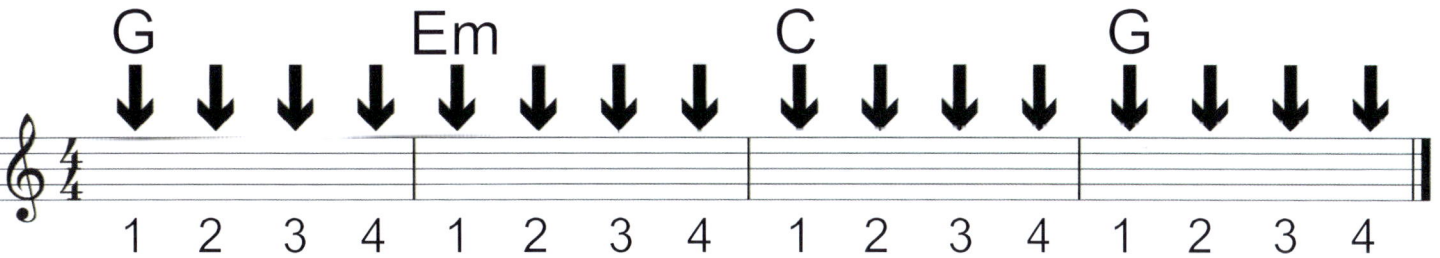

Your 1st strumming song

Buying Biscuits

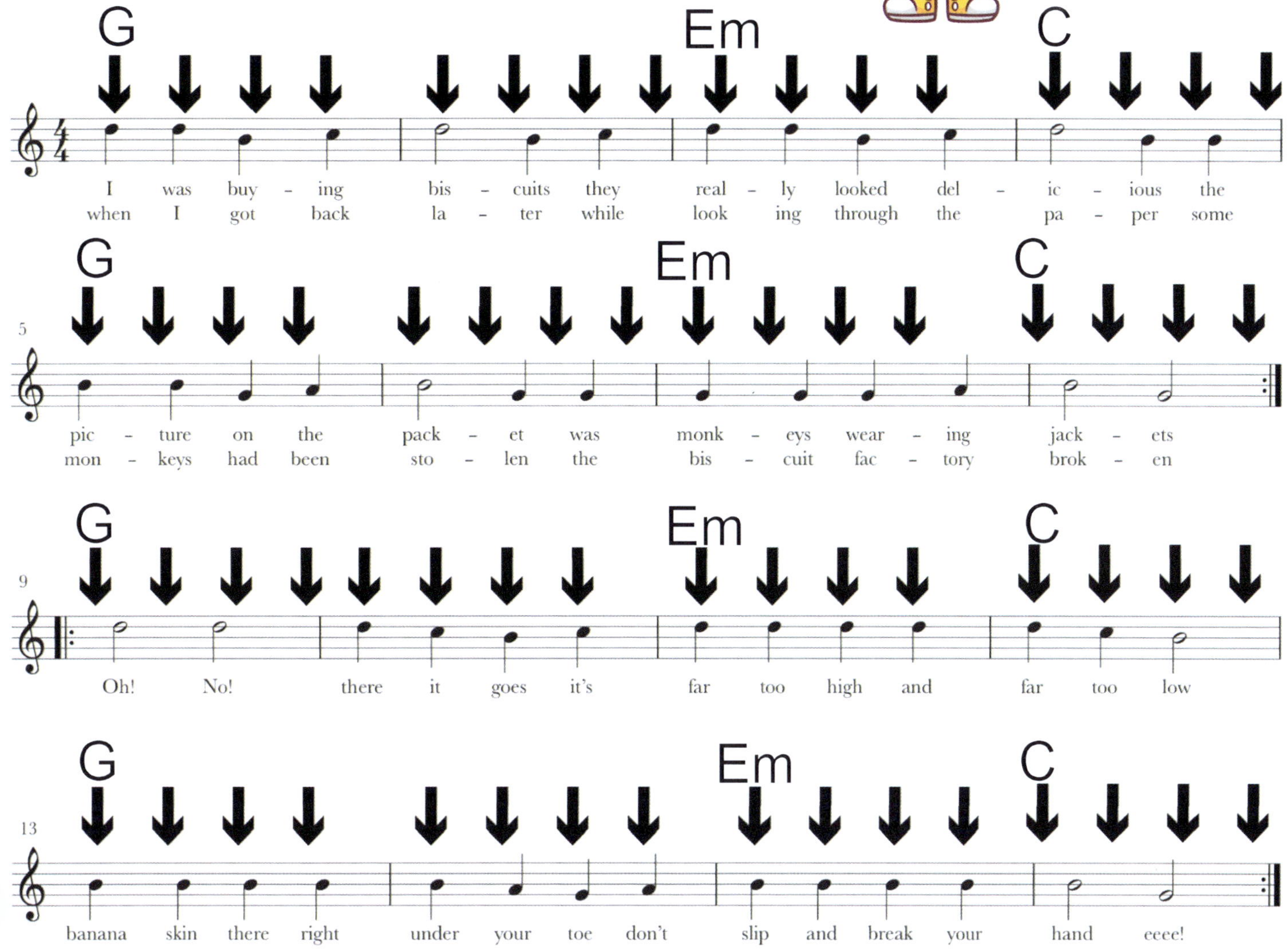

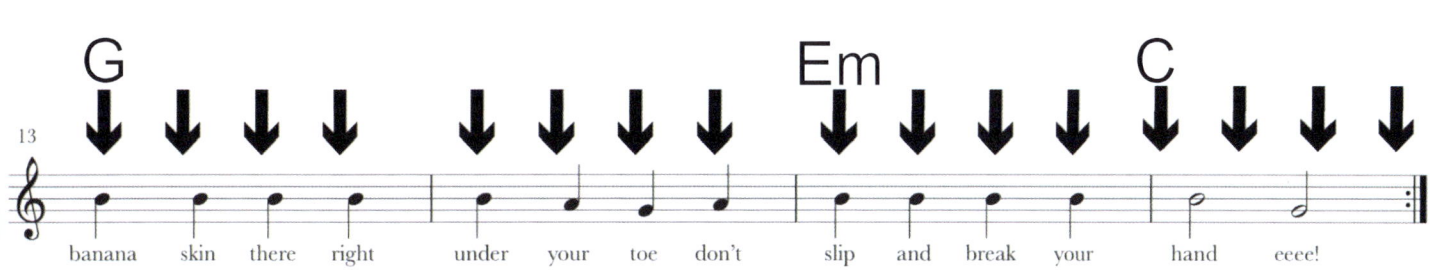

25

Three four time

Now there are three beats in a bar!

Waltzing In!

Dotted Minim

A dotted minim, also known as a dotted half note, is a note that lasts for three beats.

Ring for 3

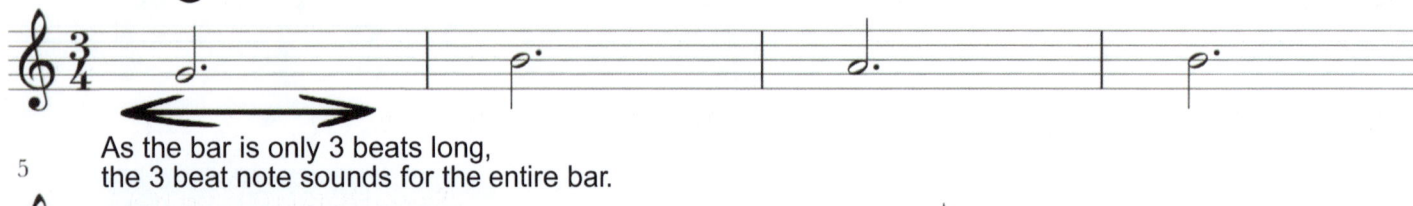

As the bar is only 3 beats long, the 3 beat note sounds for the entire bar.

Musical tie

A musical tie is a curved line that connects two of the same note to make them sound like one long note.

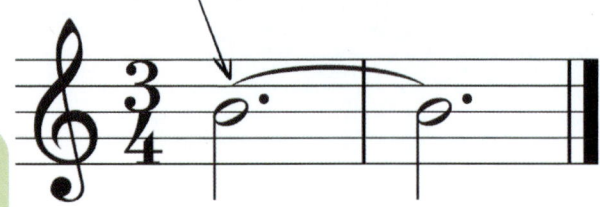

Only play the first note!

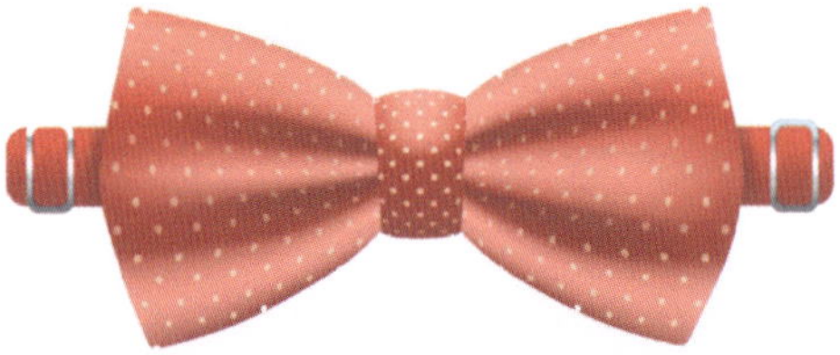

Who Ties the Tie?

Play this note

Don't replay this, just let the original note ring!

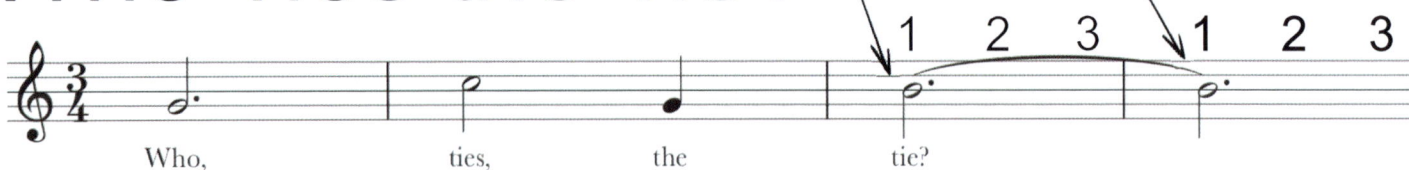

Who, ties, the tie?

Who ties the tie?

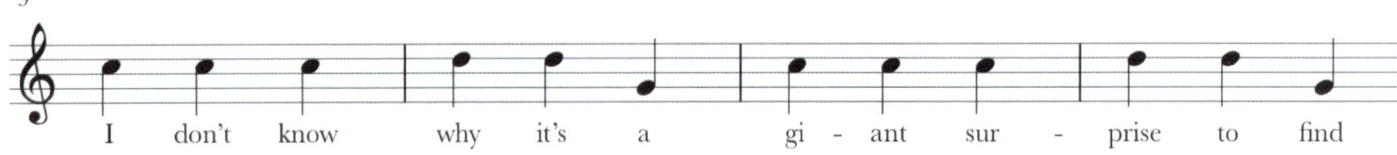

I don't know why it's a gi - ant sur - prise to find

who, ties the tie?

Quiz Question 6

How many beats in a dotted minim?

Flowers from the North

Muckle Massive

Climbing Mountains

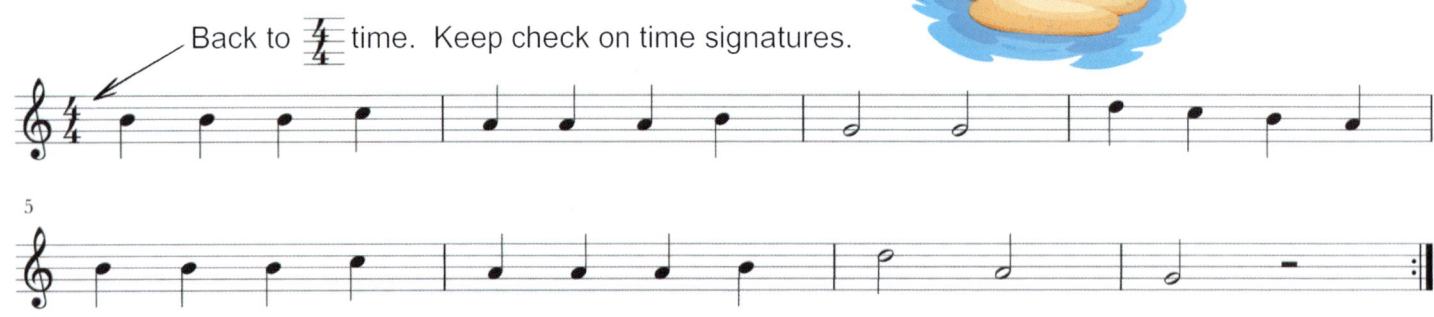

Best game Ever!

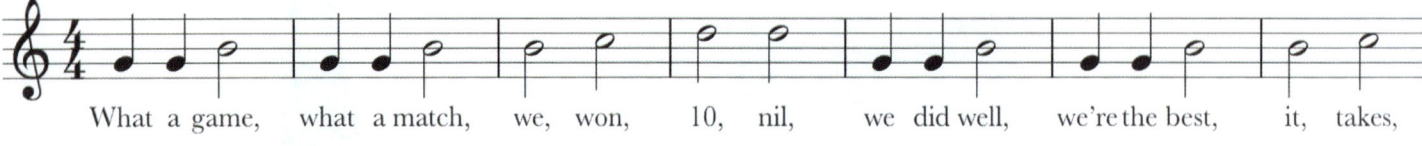
What a game, what a match, we, won, 10, nil, we did well, we're the best, it, takes,

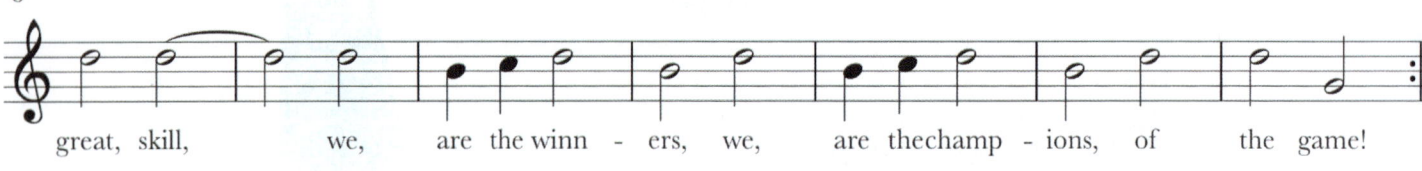
great, skill, we, are the winn - ers, we, are the champ - ions, of the game!

D Chord

D Chord

Press 1st finger on string 3, fret 2.
2nd finger on string 1 fret 2
3rd finger on string 2 fret 3

Note:
Arch your fingers over to avoid muting strings

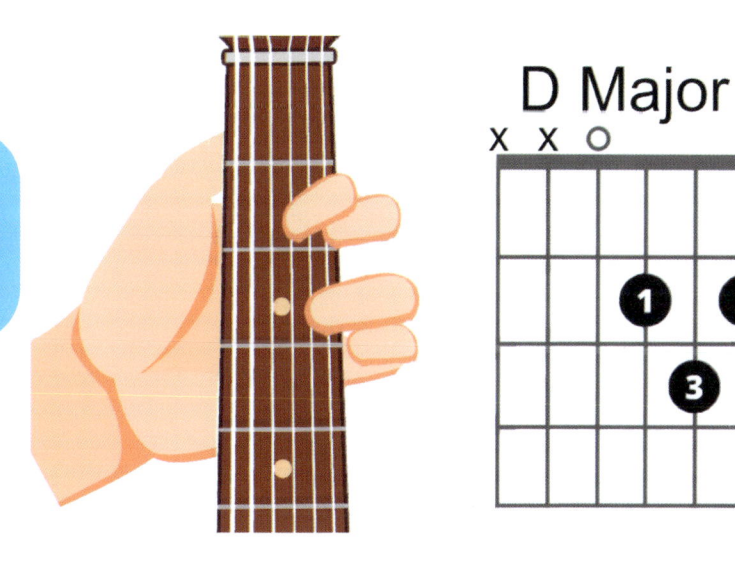

This chord is a bit trickier than the others so may need a bit of PRACTICE!

D Major

D Strum

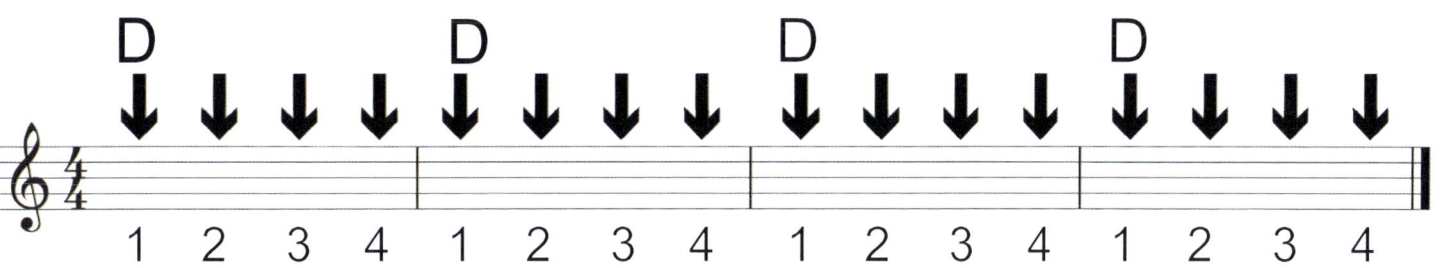

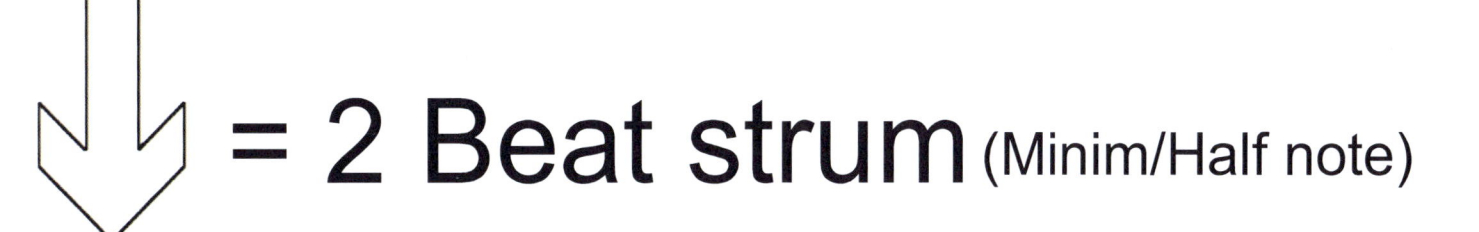

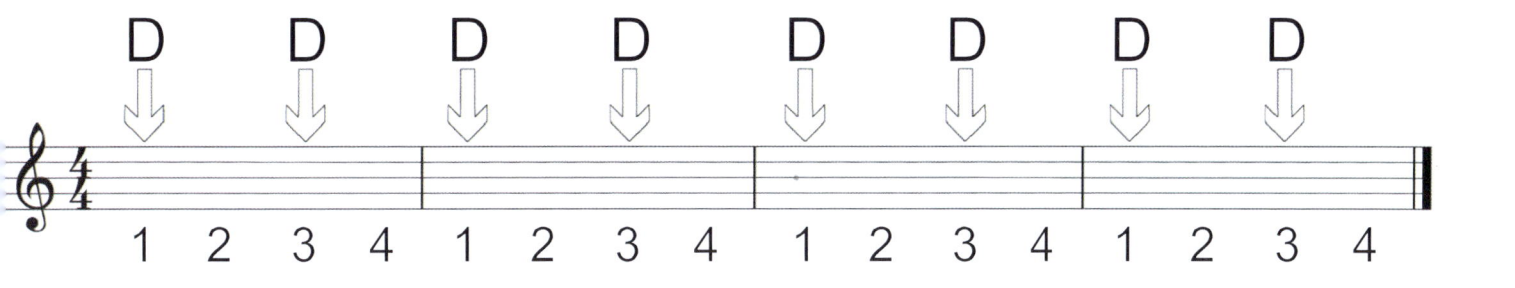

D ↓ ↓ ↓ ↓ D ↓ ↓ ↓ ↓ D ↓ ↓ ↓ ↓ D ↓ ↓ ↓ ↓

1 2 3 4 1 2 3 4 1 2 3 4 1 2 3 4

⇩ = 2 Beat strum (Minim/Half note)

D ⇩ D ⇩ D ⇩ D ⇩ D ⇩ D ⇩ D ⇩ D ⇩

1 2 3 4 1 2 3 4 1 2 3 4 1 2 3 4

The Power of 4 Chords

Now you have learned these 4 chords, there are lots of famous songs that you can play which only need these 4.

Below are 4 staves with chords above. See if you can find songs you know that sound like them.

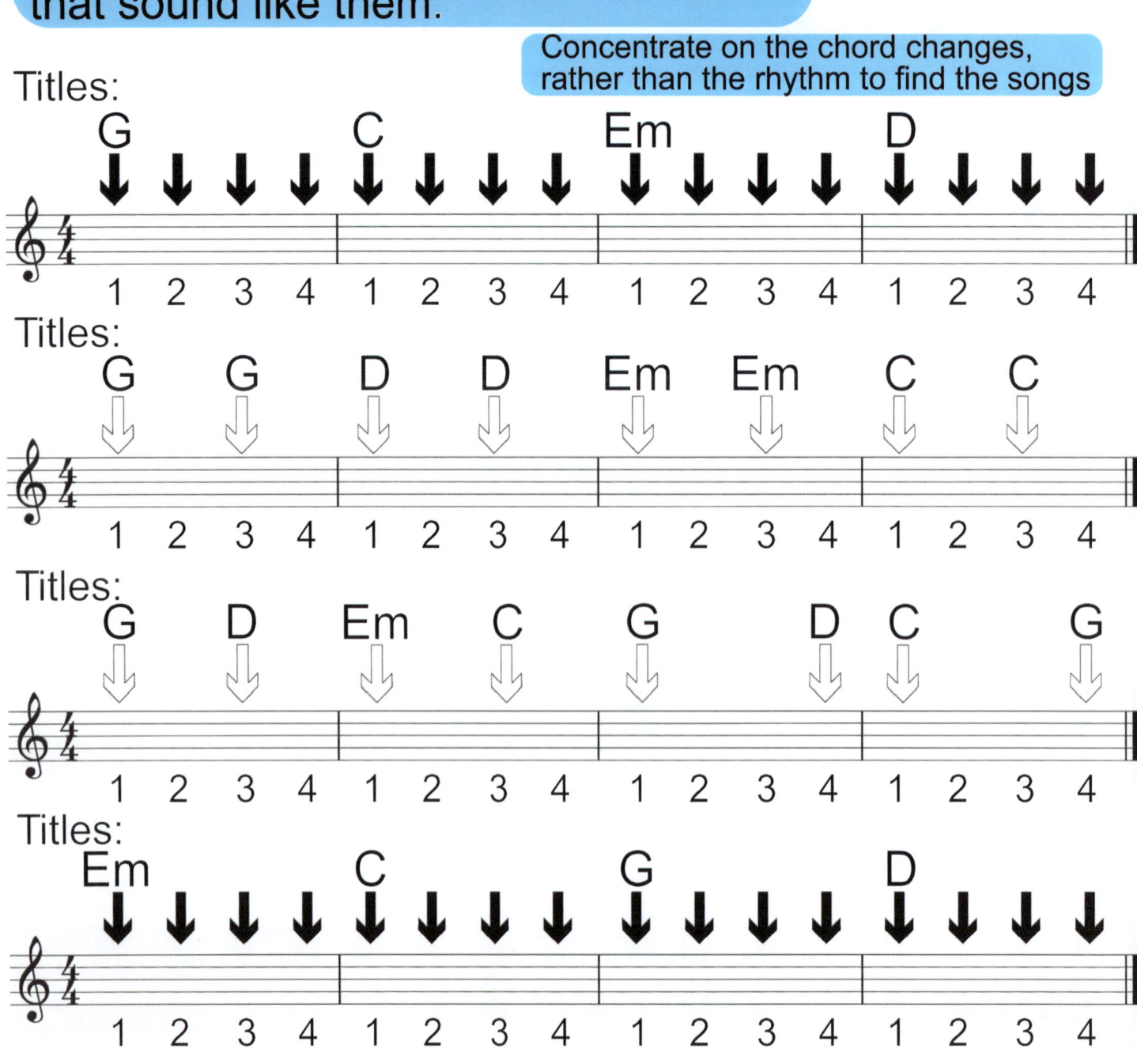

Concentrate on the chord changes, rather than the rhythm to find the songs

Titles:

G ↓ ↓ ↓ ↓ | C ↓ ↓ ↓ ↓ | Em ↓ ↓ ↓ ↓ | D ↓ ↓ ↓ ↓

1 2 3 4 | 1 2 3 4 | 1 2 3 4 | 1 2 3 4

Titles:

G G | D D | Em Em | C C

1 2 3 4 | 1 2 3 4 | 1 2 3 4 | 1 2 3 4

Titles:

G D | Em C | G D | C G

1 2 3 4 | 1 2 3 4 | 1 2 3 4 | 1 2 3 4

Titles:

Em ↓ ↓ ↓ ↓ | C ↓ ↓ ↓ ↓ | G ↓ ↓ ↓ ↓ | D ↓ ↓ ↓ ↓

1 2 3 4 | 1 2 3 4 | 1 2 3 4 | 1 2 3 4

Write Your Own

Have a go at writing your own chord progression, and make your own song!

Obviously songs are not just 4 bars long. Here are some staves to get you started.

Titles:

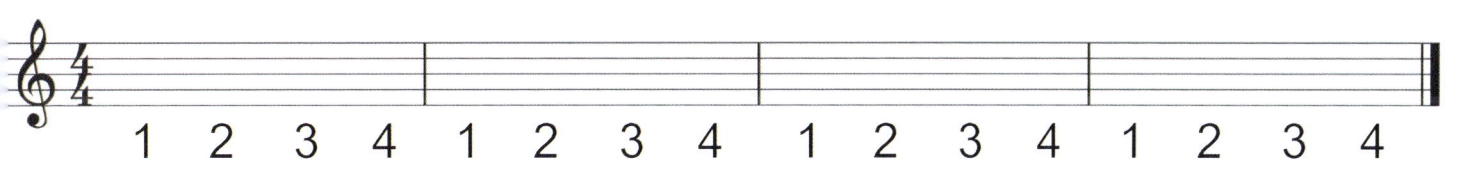

| 1 2 3 4 | 1 2 3 4 | 1 2 3 4 | 1 2 3 4 |

Lyrics:

Titles:

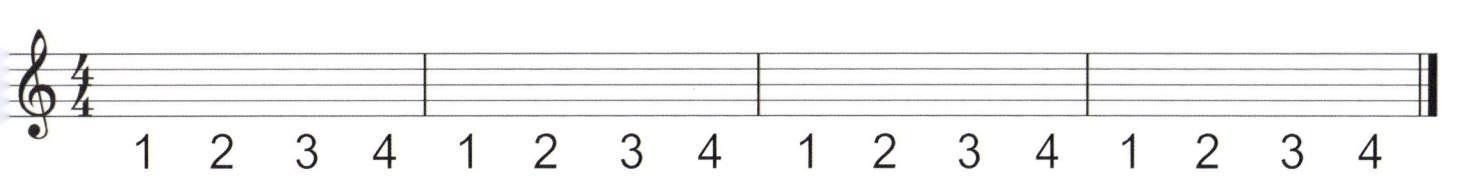

| 1 2 3 4 | 1 2 3 4 | 1 2 3 4 | 1 2 3 4 |

Lyrics:

Quiz Question 7

Which note in a tie do you not play again?

Songwriting Continued

Titles:

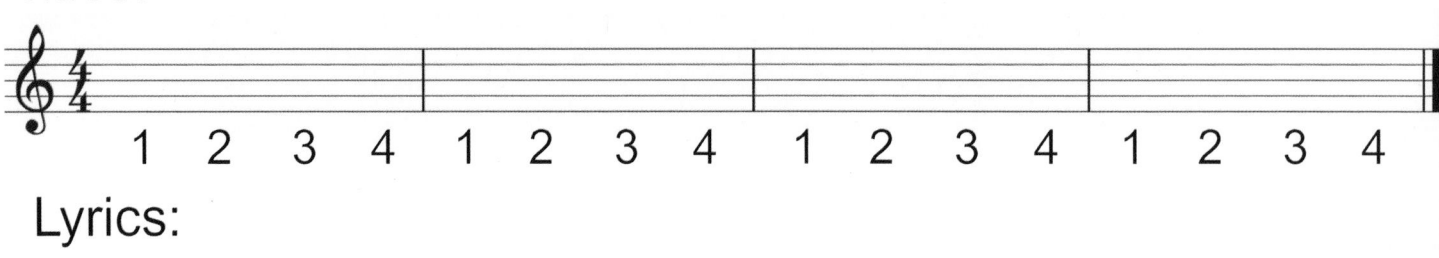

Lyrics:

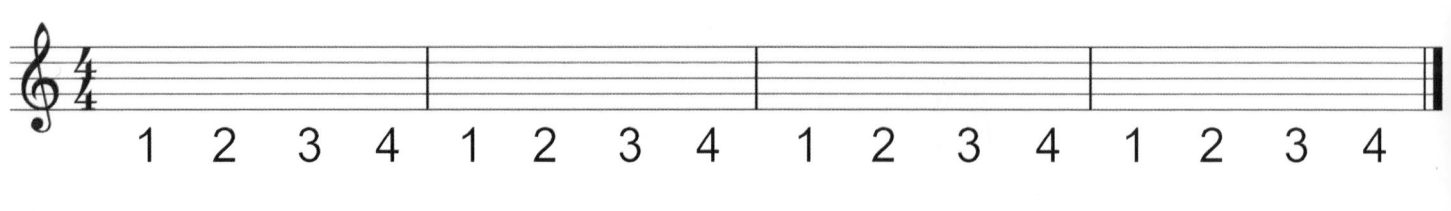

Titles:

Lyrics:

Songwriting Continued

Titles:

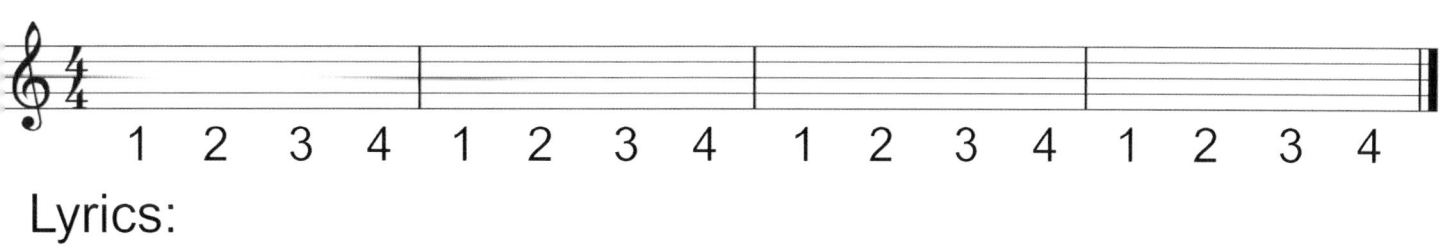

｜ 1　2　3　4　｜ 1　2　3　4　｜ 1　2　3　4　｜ 1　2　3　4 ｜

Lyrics:

Titles:

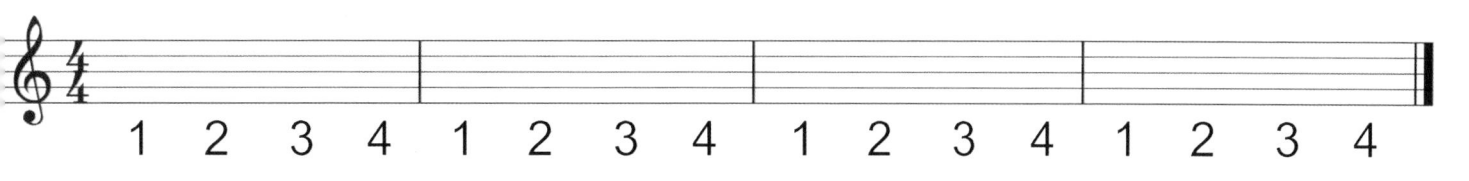

｜ 1　2　3　4　｜ 1　2　3　4　｜ 1　2　3　4　｜ 1　2　3　4 ｜

Lyrics:

TABLATURE

What is Tablature?

Tablature, commonly known as "tab" is a simplified musical notation system for guitarists. It uses numbers to show which frets to press and strings to pluck, making it easier to learn and play songs without needing to read traditional sheet music.

How does Tablature/Tab work?

The numbers tells you the frets you press. two find the string to play, count the lines down.

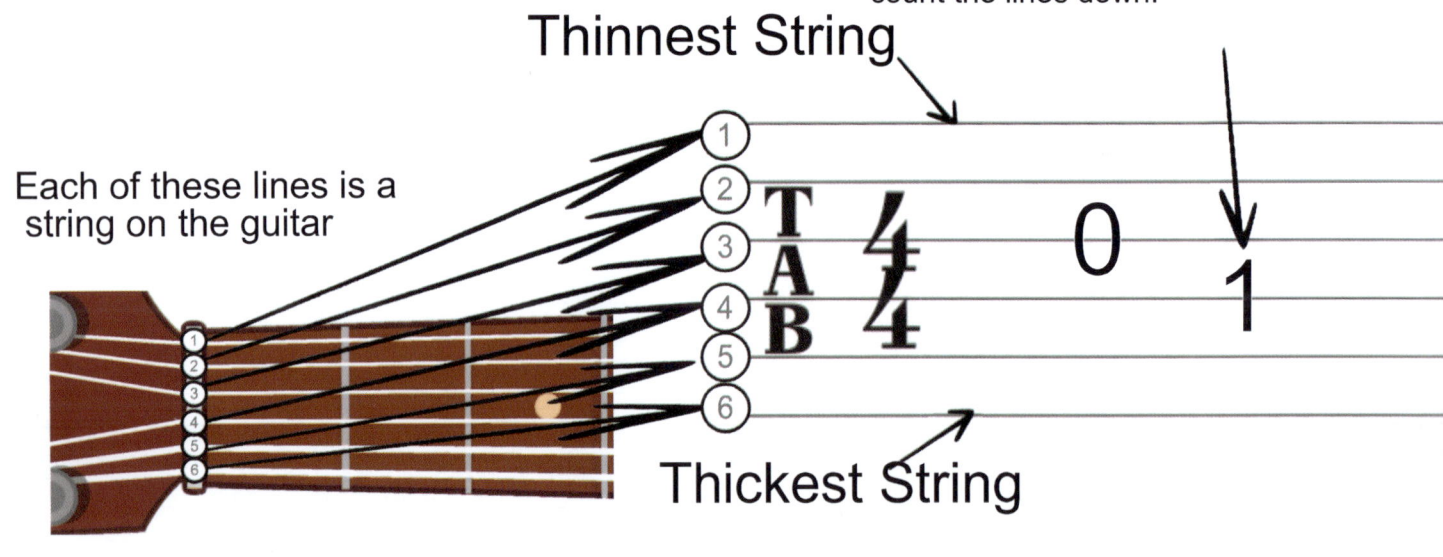

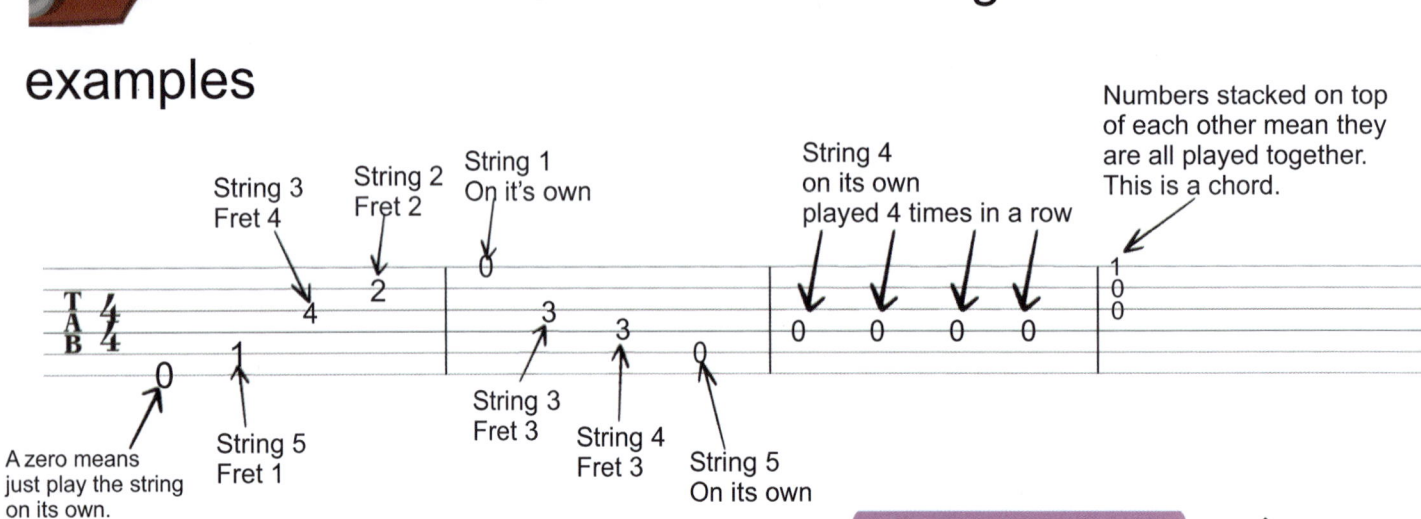

Thinnest String

Each of these lines is a string on the guitar

Thickest String

examples

String 3 Fret 4

String 2 Fret 2

String 1 On it's own

String 3 Fret 3

String 4 Fret 3

String 5 On its own

String 4 on its own played 4 times in a row

Numbers stacked on top of each other mean they are all played together. This is a chord.

A zero means just play the string on its own.

String 5 Fret 1

Quiz Question 8

What is this musical symbol

Jingle Bells

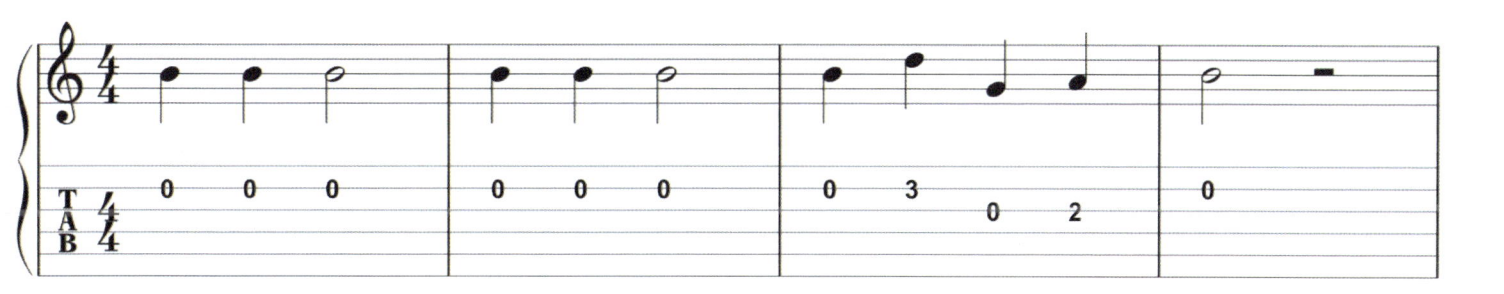

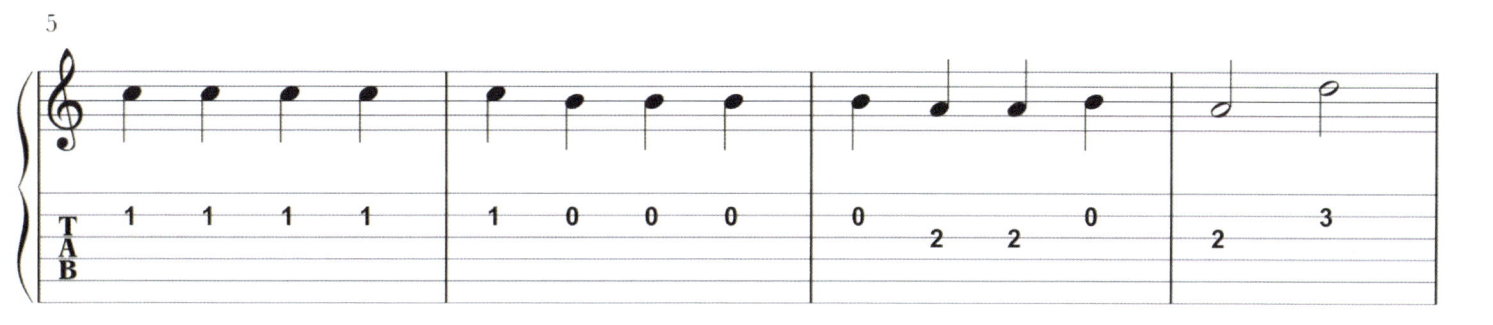

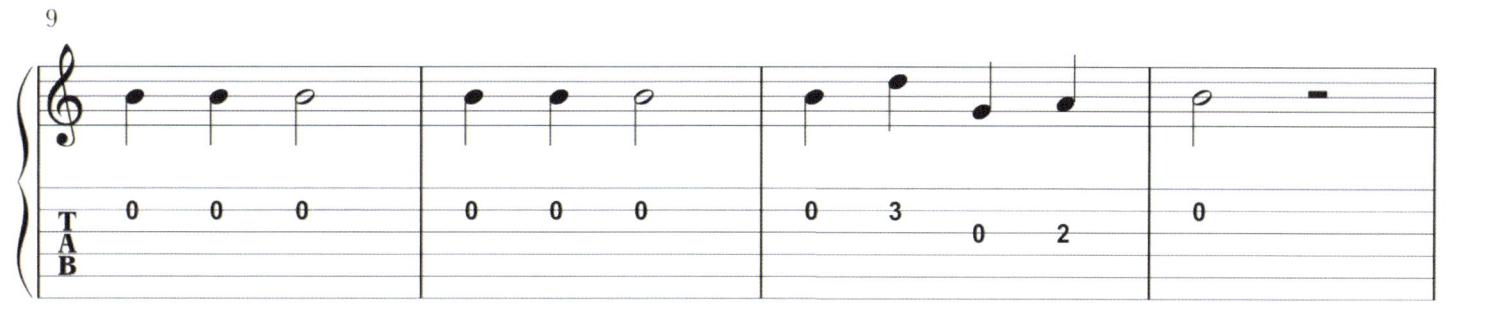

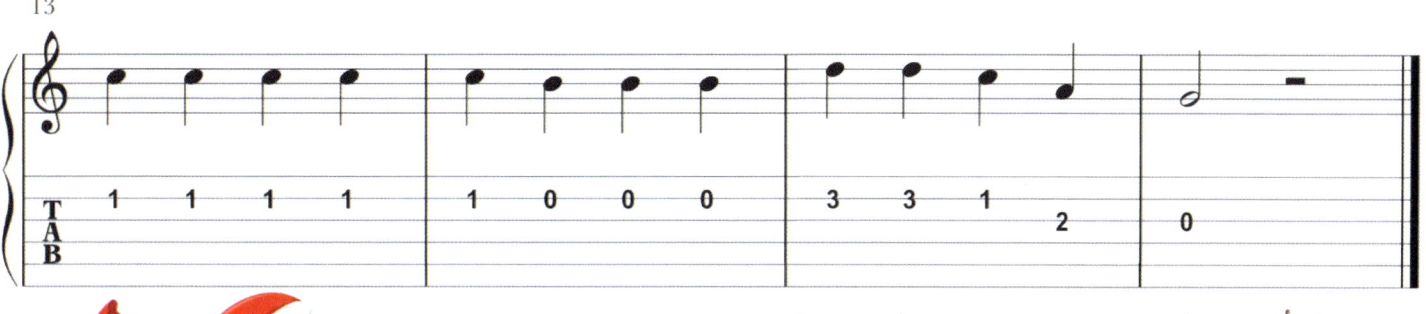

E

"E" can be found on the 4th space of The Stave.

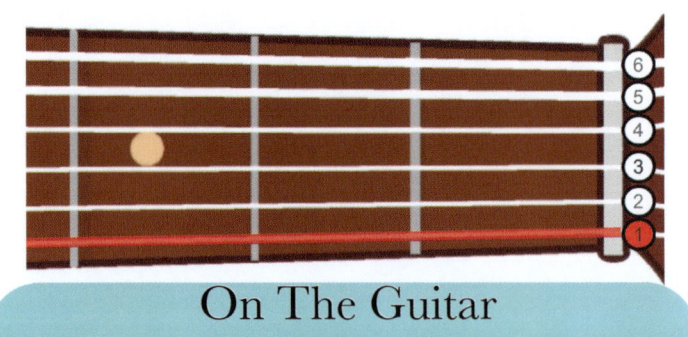

On The Guitar

The note "E" can be found by playing string 1 by itself.

Eeee!

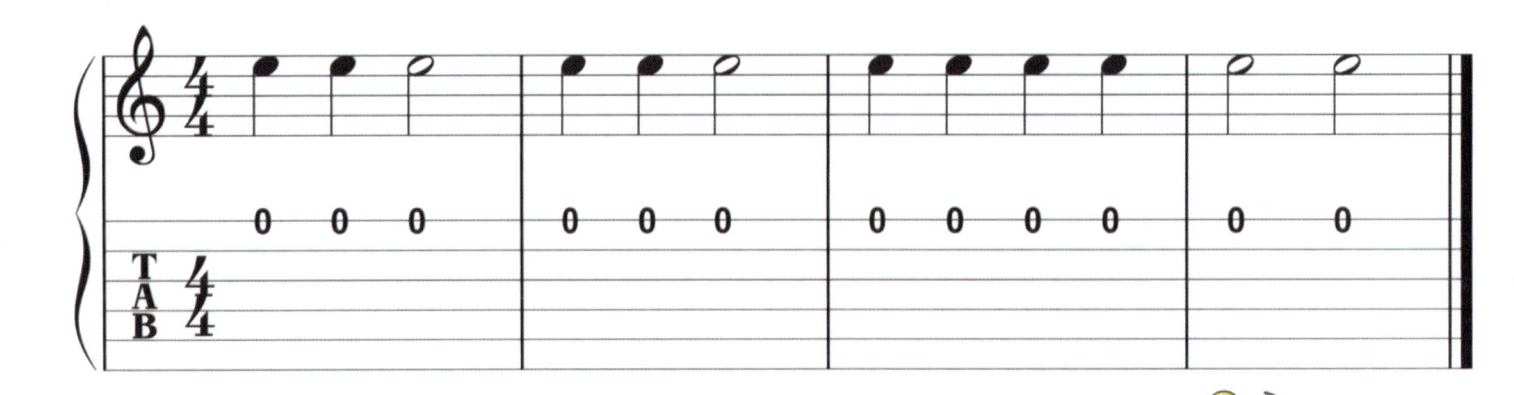

Bingo was his Name!

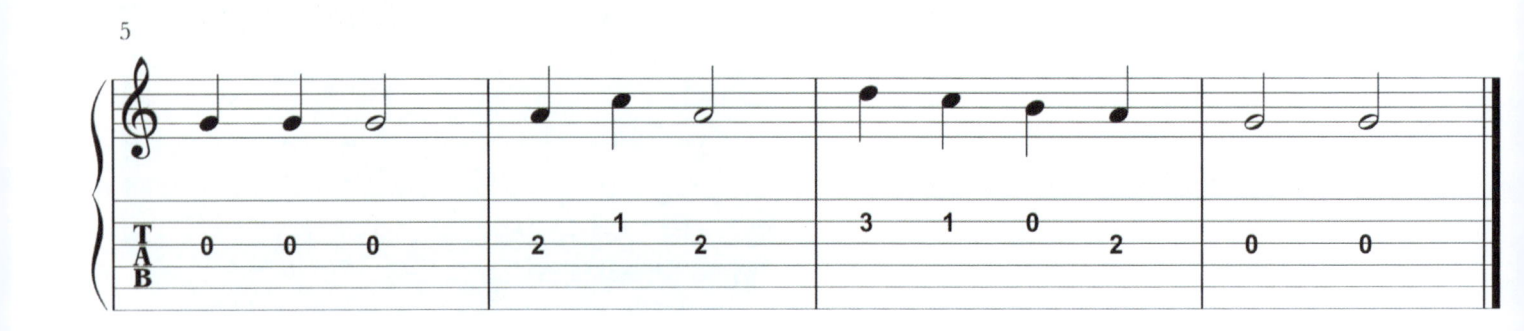

Pirates

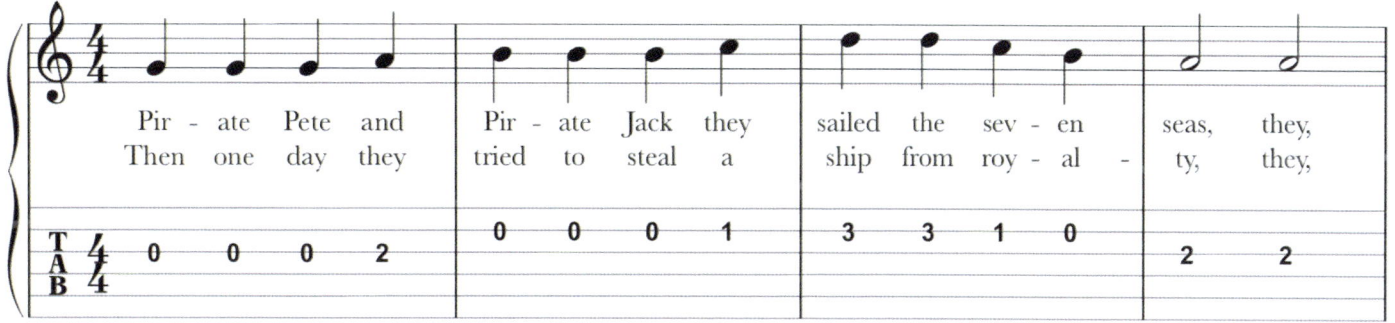

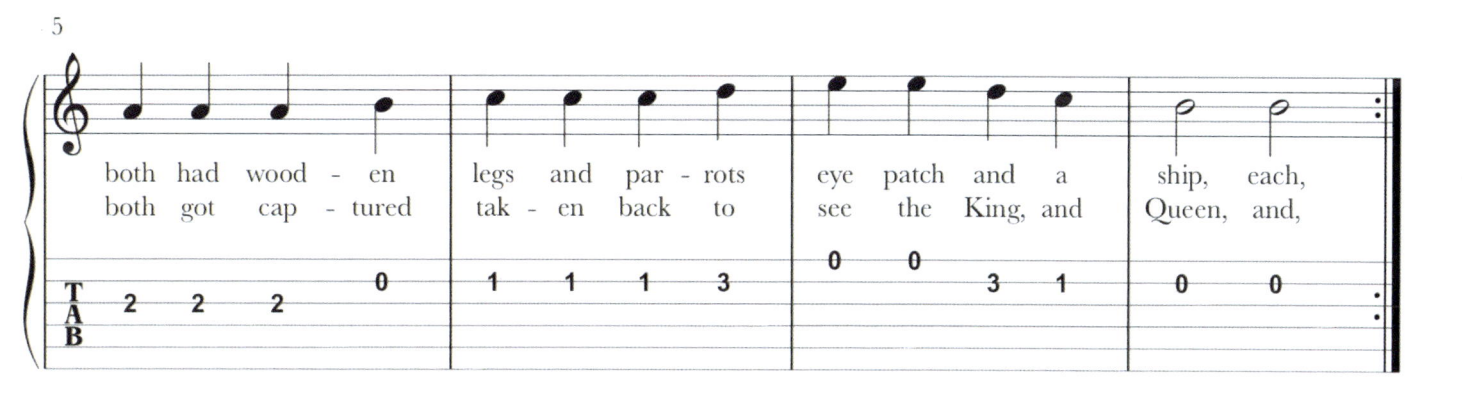

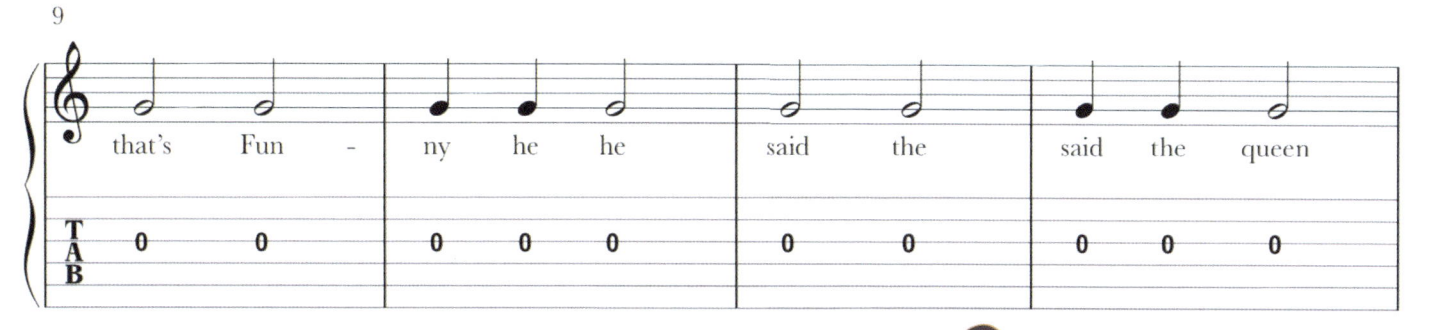

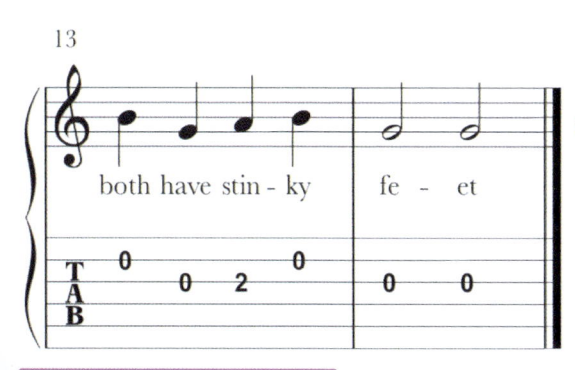

Pir - ate Pete and Pir - ate Jack they sailed the sev - en seas, they,
Then one day they tried to steal a ship from roy - al - ty, they,

both had wood - en legs and par - rots eye patch and a ship, each,
both got cap - tured tak - en back to see the King, and Queen, and,

that's Fun - ny he he said the said the queen

both have stin - ky fe - et

Quiz Question 9

What does the bar line do?

The Crotchet Rest

A crotchet rest, also known as a quarter note rest, is a symbol in music that tells the player to be quiet for one beat.

When you play a rest, release the pressure of your finger on the string but do not lift your finger off.

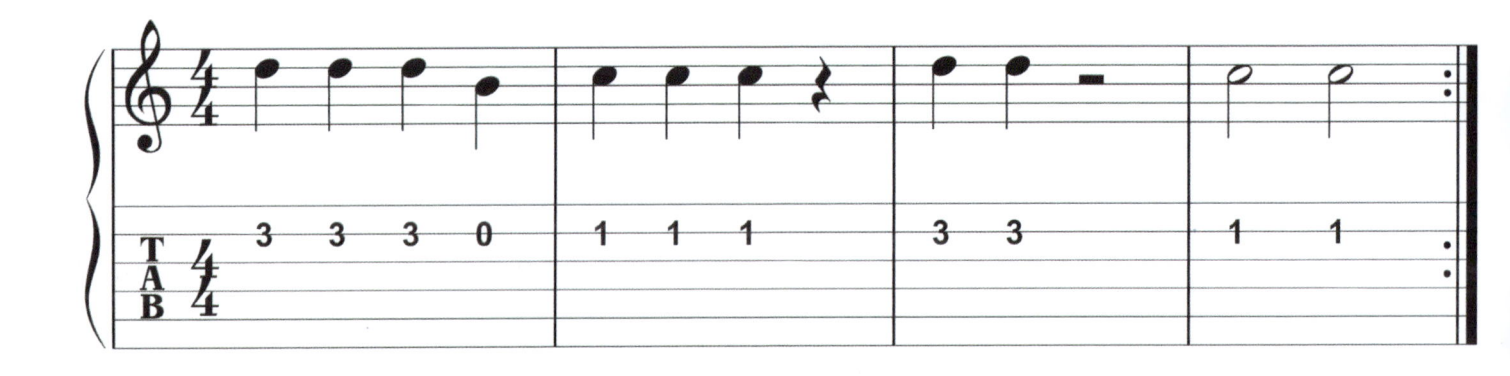

You can use the rests together

The Race

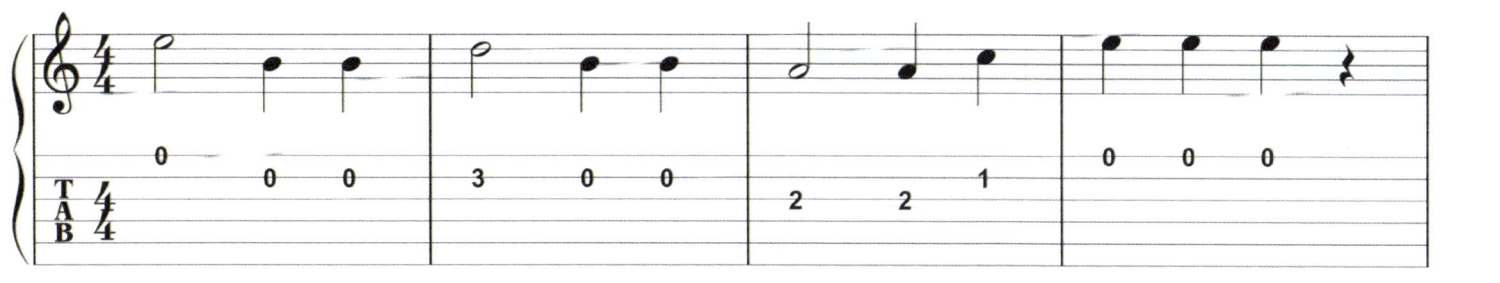

There They Go!

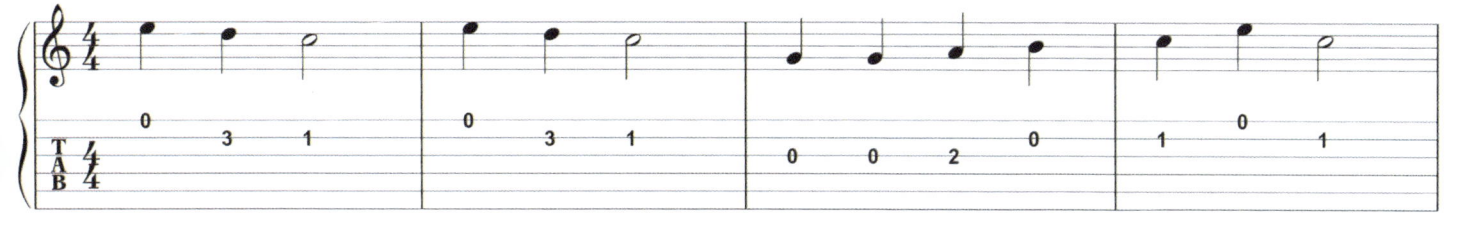

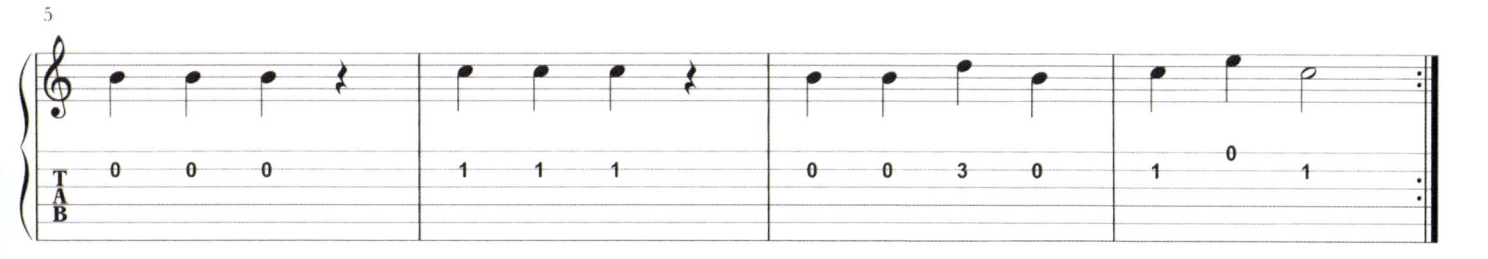

Quiz Question 10

What does the bottom number of the time signature mean?

Semibreve

A Semibreve, also known as a whole note, is a note that lasts for four beats.

The 4 beat note sounds for the entire bar.

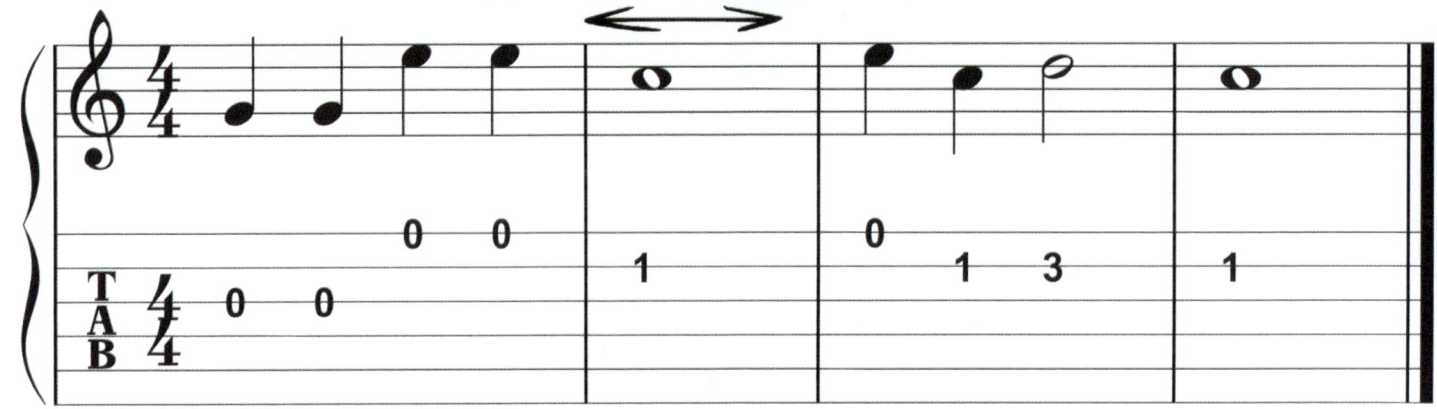

Long Time

Oh When the Saints

QUIZ Answers

Quiz Question 1

Can you name these notes?

Quiz Answers

F D A E

Find Mr A

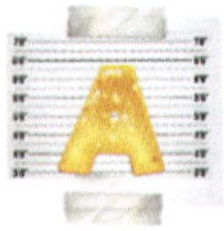

Quiz Question 2

Amongst lots of the same notes can you find the A's and G's?

Find Mr G

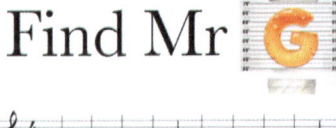

Quiz Question 3

Where can the note "B" be found on the guitar?

The note "B" is on string 2 by itself.

Quiz Question 4

What does the top number of the time signature mean?

How many beats in a bar.

Quiz Question 5

Which string on the guitar is number 1?

The thinnest string is number 1.

Quiz Question 6

How many beats in a dotted minim?

There are 3 beats in a dotted Minim.

Quiz Question 7

Which note in a tie do you not play again?

You don't play the 2nd note, you just let it ring.

Quiz Question 8

What is this musical symbol

It is called a Treble Clef.

Quiz Question 9

What does the bar line do?

The bar line separates each bar, making music easier to read.

Quiz Question 10

What does the bottom number of the time signature mean?

Which type of note receives a beat..

ABOUT THE AUTHOR

Alistair Jobson resides in the North East of England with his wife, family, and beloved dog, Indiana Bones. Throughout his upbringing, his parents provided unwavering encouragement for his musical and creative pursuits. With a teaching career spanning over 25 years, he has imparted his knowledge in both guitar and piano, some of his students having proudly gone on to become professional musicians and to work in the music industry. He firmly holds the belief that no one should be discouraged from playing an instrument.

AJ ROCK SCHOOL ACADEMY

MUSIC AWARD

THIS IS TO CERTIFY THAT

_____

HAS COMPLETED THE AJ ROCK SCHOOL ACADEMY'S STEP-BY-STEP GUITAR FOR BEGINNERS

_____ _____
DATE ISSUED   GUITAR TEACHER

AWARD
AJROCKSCHOOLACADEMY

Printed in Great Britain
by Amazon